EFFECTIVE TECHNICAL COMMUNICATION

AUTHOR (S)

Prof. Pritee Sharma
Professor
School of Humanities and Social Sciences
IIT Indore, Madhya Pradesh

Dr. Sanchita Verma
Assistant Professor Adjunct (Former)
School of Humanities and Social Sciences
IIT Indore, Madhya Pradesh

REVIEWER

Prof. Aysha Vishwamohan
Professor, Department of Humanities and Social Sciences
IIT Madras, Chennai

KHANNA BOOK PUBLISHING CO. (P) Ltd.
4C/4344, Ansari Road, Darya Ganj,
New Delhi, India

All India Council for Technical Education
Nelson Mandela Marg, Vasant Kunj,
New Delhi, India

Dear Readers,

To prevent the piracy, this book is secured with HIGH SECURITY HOLOGRAM on the front title cover. In case you don't find the hologram on the front cover title, please write us to at contact@khannabooks.com or whatsapp us at +91-99109 09320 and avail special gift voucher for yourself.

Specimen of Hologram on front Cover title:

Moreover, there is a SPECIAL DISCOUNT COUPON for you with EVERY HOLOGRAM.

How to avail this SPECIAL DISCOUNT:

Step 1: Scratch the hologram

Step 2: Under the scratch area, your "coupon code" is available

Step 3: Logon to www.khannabooks.com

Step 4: Use your "coupon code" in the shopping cart and get your copy at a special discount

Step 5: Enjoy your reading!

ISBN: 978-93-5538-786-8

Book Code: UG416EN

Effective Technical Communication

by Prof. Pritee Sharma and Dr. Sanchita Verma

First Edition: 2026

Originally Published by:

All India Council for Technical Education, Ministry of Education, GOI

Exclusively Published & Distributed by:

Khanna Book Publishing Co. (P) Ltd.

4C/4344, Ansari Road, Daryaganj,
New Delhi (INDIA)

Visit us at: **www.khannabooks.com**

Write us at: **contact@khannabooks.com**

To view complete list of books, Please scan the QR Code:	KPH

Printed in Bharat.

प्रो. टी. जी. सीताराम
अध्यक्ष
Prof. T. G. Sitharam
Chairman

सत्यमेव जयते

आज़ादी का अमृत महोत्सव

अखिल भारतीय तकनीकी शिक्षा परिषद्
(भारत सरकार का एक सांविधिक निकाय)
(शिक्षा मंत्रालय, भारत सरकार)
नेल्सन मंडेला मार्ग, वसंत कुंज, नई दिल्ली–110070
दूरभाष : 011–26131498
ई–मेल : chairman@aicte-india.org

ALL INDIA COUNCIL FOR TECHNICAL EDUCATION
(A STATUTORY BODY OF THE GOVT. OF INDIA)
(Ministry of Education, Govt. of India)
Nelson Mandela Marg, Vasant Kunj, New Delhi-110070
Phone : 011-26131498
E-mail : chairman@aicte-india.org

FOREWORD

Engineers are the backbone of any modern society. They are the ones responsible for the marvels as well as the improved quality of life across the world. Engineers have driven humanity towards greater heights in a more evolved and unprecedented manner.

The All India Council for Technical Education (AICTE), have spared no efforts towards the strengthening of the technical education in the country. AICTE is always committed towards promoting quality Technical Education to make India a modern developed nation emphasizing on the overall welfare of mankind.

An array of initiatives has been taken by AICTE in last decade which have been accelerated now by the National Education Policy (NEP) 2020. The implementation of NEP under the visionary leadership of Hon'ble Prime Minister of India envisages the provision for education in regional languages to all, thereby ensuring that every graduate becomes competent enough and is in a position to contribute towards the national growth and development through innovation & entrepreneurship.

One of the spheres where AICTE had been relentlessly working since past couple of years is providing high quality original technical contents at Under Graduate & Diploma level prepared and translated by eminent educators in various Indian languages to its aspirants. For students pursuing 2nd year of their Engineering education, AICTE has identified 87 books, which shall be translated into 12 Indian languages - Hindi, Tamil, Gujarati, Odia, Bengali, Kannada, Urdu, Punjabi, Telugu, Marathi, Assamese & Malayalam. In addition to the English medium, books in different Indian Languages are going to support the students to understand the concepts in their respective mother tongue.

On behalf of AICTE, I express sincere gratitude to all distinguished authors, reviewers and translators from the renowned institutions of high repute for their admirable contribution in a record span of time.

AICTE is confident that these outcomes based original contents shall help aspirants to master the subject with comprehension and greater ease.

(Prof. T. G. Sitharam)

ACKNOWLEDGEMENT

This work has been the most enriching experience of our lives. We are deeply grateful to the AICTE, New Delhi and special mention goes to Prof. T. G. Sitharam, Chairman; Dr. Abhay Jere, Vice-Chairman; Prof. Rajive Kumar, Member-Secretary; and Dr. Sunil Luthra, Director, Training and Learning Bureau. Their collective vision and planning were instrumental in the publication of the book on *Effective Technical Communication*.

We express our deep gratitude to Professor Aysha Vishwamohan, Department of Humanities and Social Sciences, IIT Madras for making timely and invaluable contribution in reviewing this book. Her suggestions have helped us in shaping this book to its present form.

We extend our heartfelt thanks to colleagues, faculty members and staff members of School of Humanities and Social Sciences, IIT Indore. Our discussions and critical comments received on the manuscript have helped us in making this book reader friendly.

A special thanks goes to our family members, our respective spouses and children who have been very patient and understanding during the preparation of the book. Without their help, this book could not have been written.

Thanks is also due to Dinabandhu and Amrutha, IIT Indore and Madan Mohan, NIEPA, New Delhi who helped us with the technical aspects of preparing the manuscript.

Last but not least, we express our heartfelt gratitude to our students who have helped us to reflect and shape our thoughts. We have learnt a lot from the classroom interactions, their questions and interventions.

This book is an outcome of various suggestions of AICTE members, experts and authors who shared their opinions and thoughts from time to time. Acknowledgements are due to different authors and stakeholders in the field whose published books, articles, papers and references have enriched us while writing this book.

Prof. Pritee Sharma

Dr. Sanchita Verma

PREFACE

In contemporary times, the world of technical communication has become structured and complex. The organisations are increasingly becoming multinational and multicultural, not just in terms of business but workforce too. Hence the communication pattern and demands vis-à-vis organisations and institutions is also evolving. This book will bridge the huge gap in technical communication between what we learn as students and how we perform as part of the workforce in an organisation.

The book commences with the detailed explanation of communication as a process providing a conceptual framework for rest of the units. It explains the principle, process and purpose of the technical communication and its importance in our daily lives.

As readers progress further they will find a detailed description of not just the communication process but routine technical correspondence, oral business communication, e-communication and planning and preparing organizational documents.

The book provides updated information on the relevant topics with QR code for further learning. It has been written with a student centric approach and they will find it very useful to understand different concepts.

We hope this book will be an invaluable resource for students, teachers, educators, other stakeholders and general readers.

We welcome valuable suggestions and feedback to improve this book.

Prof. Pritee Sharma

Dr. Sanchita Verma

OUTCOME-BASED EDUCATION

For the implementation of outcome based education the first requirement is to develop an outcome based curriculum and incorporate an outcome based assessment in the education system. By going through outcome based assessments evaluators will be able to evaluate whether the students have achieved the outlined standard with specific and measurable outcomes. With the proper incorporation of outcome based education there will be a definite commitment to achieve a minimum standard for all learners without giving up at any level. At the end of the programme running with the aid of outcome based education, a student will be able to arrive at the following outcomes:

PO1. Engineering knowledge: Apply the knowledge of mathematics, science, engineering fundamentals, and an engineering specialization to the solution of complex engineering problems.

PO2. Problem analysis: Identify, formulate, review research literature, and analyze complex engineering problems reaching substantiated conclusions using first principles of mathematics, natural sciences, and engineering sciences.

PO3. Design / development of solutions: Design solutions for complex engineering problems and design system components or processes that meet the specified needs with appropriate consideration for the public health and safety, and the cultural, societal, and environmental considerations.

PO4. Conduct investigations of complex problems: Use research-based knowledge and research methods including design of experiments, analysis and interpretation of data, and synthesis of the information to provide valid conclusions.

PO5. Modern tool usage: Create, select, and apply appropriate techniques, resources, and modern engineering and IT tools including prediction and modeling to complex engineering activities with an understanding of the limitations.

PO6. The engineer and society: Apply reasoning informed by the contextual knowledge to assess societal, health, safety, legal and cultural issues and the consequent responsibilities relevant to the professional engineering practice.

PO7. Environment and sustainability: Understand the impact of the professional engineering solutions in societal and environmental contexts, and demonstrate the knowledge of, and need for sustainable development.

PO8. Ethics: Apply ethical principles and commit to professional ethics and responsibilities and norms of the engineering practice.

PO9. Individual and team work: Function effectively as an individual, and as a member or leader in diverse teams, and in multidisciplinary settings.

PO10. Communication: Communicate effectively on complex engineering activities with the engineering community and with society at large, such as, being able to comprehend and write effective reports and design documentation, make effective presentations, and give and receive clear instructions.

PO11. Project management and finance: Demonstrate knowledge and understanding of the engineering and management principles and apply these to one's own work, as a member and leader in a team, to manage projects and in multidisciplinary environments.

PO12. Life-long learning: Recognize the need for, and have the preparation and ability to engage in independent and life-long learning in the broadest context of technological change.

COURSE OUTCOMES

By the completion of the course, students should learn:

CO-1: To develop and exhibit effective oral communication skills appropriate for technical situations/interactions.

CO-2: To create well-structured and coherent written technical documents, such as reports, manuals, and technical communication, using proper forms and styles.

CO-3: To customize communication strategies for different audiences, ensuring that technical and non-technical stakeholders can comprehend and interact with the content.

CO-4: To demonstrate superior listening skills and give constructive feedback to promote good interpersonal and team communication.

CO-5: To use nonverbal communication skills to increase the impact and clarity of communication during presentations and conversations.

CO-6: To use new digital tools and technology to assist and improve their communication activities while maintaining efficiency and professionalism.

Mapping of Course Outcomes with Programme Outcomes to be done according to the matrix given below:

Course Outcomes	PO-1	PO-2	PO-3	PO-4	PO-5	PO-6	PO-7	PO-8
CO-1	3	1	2	2	2	2	2	2
CO-2	3	3	2	1	1	2	3	2
CO-3	3	2	3	2	2	2	2	2
CO-4	3	1	2	3	2	2	2	2
CO-5	2	1	3	2	3	2	2	2
CO-6	2	2	2	1	1	3	3	3

(Note: 1- Weak Correlation; 2- Medium Correlation; 3- Strong Correlation)

GUIDELINES FOR TEACHERS

Objective

To enhance students' knowledge and skills in communication techniques as part of an effective communication curriculum. Teachers should strive to provide students with the skills to communicate clearly and successfully in diverse professional situations.

Teacher's Responsibilities

- Allocate time effectively to each unit to ensure all students grasp key communication concepts. Assess the students based on defined criteria related to technical communication skills.
- Improve students' learning and communication skills for professional usage.
- Ensure students are skilled appropriately in verbal and nonverbal communication after completing the course.
- Encourage students to develop their communication performance capabilities.
- Facilitate and promote group work and teamwork to practice communication in diverse settings.
- Follow Bloom's Taxonomy in assessing students' technical communication skills.

Bloom's Taxonomy:

Level	Teacher should check	Student should be able to	Possible mode of assessment
Create	Students' ability to create	Design or create	Develop a comprehensive communication plan
Evaluate	Students' ability to justify	Argue or defend	Write and defend a communication strategy
Analyze	Students' ability to distinguish	Differentiate or distinguish	Analyse case studies on communication issues
Apply	Students' ability to use information	Operate or demonstrate	Present technical information effectively
Understand	Students' ability to explain ideas	Explain or classify	Conduct presentations or seminars
Remember	Students' ability to recall	Define or Recall	Quiz on communication theories and concepts

GUIDELINES FOR STUDENTS

To learn technical communication, students should share equal responsibility of mastering communication techniques. Some of the responsibilities (not limited to) for the students in mastering communication techniques are as follows:

- Students should be aware of the key concepts and objectives of each chapter before starting a unit.
- Students should be aware of the specific outcomes expected from each chapter before the start of the unit.
- Students should think critically and rationally with proper reflection and action regarding their communication practices.
- The students' learning should be integrated with practical and real-life communication scenarios.
- Students should be continuously aware of their competency levels in different dimensions of communication.

LIST OF FIGURES, TABLES AND FORMATS

TABLE OF CONTENTS

1 Introduction to the Essentials of Technical Communication

Unit Specifics

At the centre of our study of communication is the relationship that involves interaction between participants. This can be understood through the concept of process, understanding, sharing, and meaning.

The first word ***process*** *is a dynamic activity which continuously changes and keeps evolving between the participants. Imagine you are reading something in your room and your mother enters and you talk briefly. What has changed? Now, imagine that your mother is joined by someone else, someone you have not met before – and this stranger is listening as you are speaking, almost as if you were giving a speech. What has changed? Your perspective might change, and you might watch your words more closely. The feedback or response from your mother and the stranger (who are your audience) may cause you to revaluate what you are saying.* ***When we interact, all these factors—and many more—influence the process of communication.***

The second key word is ***understanding****: "To understand is to perceive, to interpret, and to relate our perception and interpretation to what we already know." (McLean, 2003) If your grandmother tells you a story about falling off the staircase, what image comes to your mind? Now your grandmother points out to the spot where you see someone lying on the ground.* ***Understanding the words and the concepts or objects they refer to is an important part of the communication process.***

Next comes the word ***sharing*** *which is doing something together with one or more people. You may share a joint activity, when you are doing a group assignment; or you may benefit jointly from a resource, when your group is sharing a report accessed from the library.* ***In communication, sharing occurs when you convey thoughts, feelings, ideas, or insights to others****. You can also share with yourself (a process called intrapersonal communication) when you bring ideas to consciousness, ponder how you feel about something, or figure out the solution to a problem when something becomes clear.*

Finally, ***meaning*** *is what we share through communication. The derived meaning can sometimes be ambiguous.* ***By looking at the context and the discourse where the word has been used and by asking questions, we can discover the shared meaning of the word and understand the message.***

Apart from this at the end of the unit, a succinct recapitulation of the overall broad concepts is provided in the form of unit summary. Besides, a large number of multiple-choice questions as well as descriptive type questions are included. A list of references and suggested readings are given in the unit so that one can go through them for practice. It is important to note that for getting more information on various topics of interest some QR codes have been provided which can be scanned for relevant knowledge. Video resources along with QR codes are mentioned for getting more information on various topics of interest which can be surfed or scanned through mobile phones for viewing.

Rationale

Communication is an everyday activity. It is so natural and innate to us that we hardly ever take a pause to understand this process communication. It is a complex network of encoding, sending, decoding, feedback and response mechanisms. It is important for students to understand and appreciate this mundane and routine activity for its process, diversity and complexity.

Pre-requisites

Before reading this unit, the students are advised to revisit the following:

Employability Skills Class XII, Chapter 1 Communication Skills, NCERT

Basic Idea of Listening-Speaking-Reading-Writing, henceforth (LSRW) Skills

Unit Outcomes

U1-O1 *Understand communication- system and process.*

U1-O2 *Develop LSRW Skills*

U1-O3 *Apply cultural dimensions and communication practices for effective cross-cultural interactions.*

U1-O4 *Develop and apply diversity and gender-sensitive policies to ensure equal opportunities.*

U1-O5 *Challenge and overcome gender stereotypes to foster an inclusive work environment.*

U1-O6 *Improve communication and team dynamics by applying gender sensitivity and cultural understanding.*

Unit-1 Outcomes	EXPECTED MAPPING WITH COURSE OUTCOMES (1- Weak Correlation; 2- Medium correlation; 3- Strong Correlation)					
	CO-1	CO-2	CO-3	CO-4	CO-5	CO-6
U1-O1	2	1	3	2	2	2
U1-O2	1	2	3	2	1	2
U1-O3	1	2	2	1	1	1
U1-O4	1	1	2	1	1	1
U1-O5	2	1	2	2	2	1
U1-O6	2	1	3	3	2	2

What is Communication

Defining Communication

The root of the word "communication" in Latin is *communicare*, which means to share, or to make common (Weekley, 1967). Communication is defined as the process of understanding and sharing meaning (Pearson & Nelson, 2000). Communication is also a process of transmitting and receiving verbal and non-verbal messages. It is considered effective when it achieves the desired reaction or response from the receiver. Simply stated, communication is a two-way process of exchanging ideas or information. (Murphy et al 2000). It is the means by which behaviour is modified, change is affected, information is made productive and goals are achieved. (*Koonz et al, 1984*)

1.1 Introduction

Let us understand this concept through this analogy:

All of us share a common faculty, that is the ability to communicate and share our thoughts and intentions, and make the privacy of our thoughts public and common. From the definition of the communication mentioned above we can also say that ***communication is an essential part of our individual necessity to become a part of the domain of the common.***

Let us understand this through another example. When a child is born, the first cry communicates the sign of life to us. As an infant the same cry becomes loaded with different communicative contents, be it hunger, pain, sleep, desire for nappy change and much more. In the next phase, the child starts to communicate in monosyllables, ma-ma, da-da, pa-pa sounds which assume significance during this period of growth. Apart from these monosyllables, a child communicates through several gestures and movements too in the absence of a fully developed system of language. And, as the faculty of communication develops, the child becomes a social being who can express thoughts and needs not only to the parents but teachers, relatives, peers, and others. In this way words are constantly added to the vocabulary of the child. But communication is not just knowing words. It is more about the use and functions of words to express oneself. ***But is it enough to know the use and functions of words to communicate?***

Communication includes an entire range of media at our disposal in our effort to transfer a message and it includes components of verbal, non-verbal and body language too. It is important in the study of communication to not only include the speaker, writer, and sender, but also, the role of the listener, reader, and receiver in decoding a message.

Not just in personal or routine context, the importance of communication is manifold in an organisation also. According to organizational communications expert, Chester I Bernard, 'communication is the means by which people are linked together in an organisation to achieve a common purpose. Communication helps in giving shape to organizational goals by putting forth the objectives to be achieved and helping the employees to share a common purpose.'

If the organisation is to be viewed as a social system, then it would be viewed in terms of a communication network, where a dynamic web of vertical, lateral, and crosswise communication creates the operational structure for decision making, decision dissemination and decision implementation. Communication also facilitates business goals in the external environment through exchanges between the organisation and other agencies: customers, suppliers, stockholders, government and civic agencies, facility providers, banks and other financial organisation, embassies, and others.

Since, we are aware of the word communication and its practical importance in our lives, now we shall now learn how the communication cycle operates. A communication cycle is a complete journey of a message from encoding to decoding. Let us see the different steps involved in this cycle.

1.2 The Communication Cycle

Process: The process of communication has the following basic components that operates within a particular context: sender, encoding, medium/message, decoding, receiver, and feedback.

Sender The sender is the initiator of the communication process. S/he is the person who feels the need to communicate and express certain ideas or thoughts in her/his mind prompted by the context in which the need to communicate arises. The prompting could also be some external and /or internal stimuli. The sender's communicative environment must not only have reasons to communicate but must also have the medium in which ideas and thoughts could be encoded. The choice of medium is guided by availability of the opportunity of use of that medium by the receiver.

For example, the sender, may choose to speak to a distant receiver if s/he has access to a telephone but only when the receiver too has a phone. S/he may speak in English if the receiver understands that language, the sender must choose the appropriate words to encode the thoughts so that the receiver can understand the message. The encoding must convey the proper meaning so that the desired feedback can be elicited from the receiver. In this scenario, the sender as originator and transmitter of the message has the responsibility of forming appropriate codes, keeping in mind several circumstances that surround the communication process.

Encoding The Encoding is the process by which the senders translate their thoughts and ideas in to appropriate messages, using the medium that is shared between the sender and the receiver. Encoding is guided by sender's own communication skills as also their own estimate of the receivers' skills of comprehension. Encoding is in a way, a method of providing a structured message using a shared codes of communication that may be verbal or non-verbal. It is like giving substance to the abstraction of ideas, or providing logical codes of language systems to the unformulated ideas in the mind. The effectiveness of encoding determines the quality of the message that ultimately gets tested by receiver's comprehension of the message.

Medium/Message The encoding prepares the message in a particular medium that would enable the receiver to decode and understand the original idea that the sender wants to convey. The medium is a system of codes and signs that have a determinable meaning system that is shared between the sender and the receiver. The transference of message must necessarily depend on some medium, or else the message can neither be encoded nor sent.

The message is like water and the medium (words, gestures, signs, etc) is the container in which the message is to be transferred. In addition to the medium, the message is also sent through a channel. To use the image of water again, channel is like the water pipe that connects water from one point to another. The medium is determined by the requirements of the message, the availability of channels, the communicative skills, and the circumstances of the receiver.

Decoding Once the message reaches the receiver, it can serve its communicative purpose only if it is understood. Decoding is this process of comprehending the sense and meaning of the message so that it registers in the mind of the receiver as an understandable idea. Decoding depends on the comprehension skills of the receiver as also the quality of encoding of the sender. Furthermore, the reception of the message is better if there is no or few interferences in the transmittal. Interferences or noise as it is referred to, in the oral communicative context, reduces the quality of the incoming message and may lead to faulty decoding.

It may be remembered that there is always a possibility of transmission losses that occur when a message travels. One reason is that the meaning intended in the process of encoding may not be the same as in decoding. Misinterpretations always occurs due to the inadequate knowledge of the code. Interference may add further losses to the decoding process.

Receiver The receiver should be receptive to the message, that is s/he should be alert, attentive to multiple signals and perceptive particularly to the nonverbal media that often accompanies the verbal medium. In case of oral communication, the receiver must listen with care since sound signals exists only momentarily. The receiver's cooperation in the communication process is essential or else the exchange itself will be at stake.

The receiver's skill of comprehension of the message is another important factor in the success of the process. The sender and the receiver must share the medium of exchange and attach similar set of meaning to the words and symbols in their respective encoding and decoding. Avoiding ambiguity is another principle that helps the message to be decoded properly. Often a mix of media helps in eliminating misunderstanding, for example, when body language conveys meaning along-side oral communication.

Feedback The communication cycle remains incomplete in the absence of a feedback. The receiver's response to the message is then encoded as the feedback message for the sender. **The receiver's feedback becomes, in effect, a reversal of the communication process where the receiver becomes the sender and the sender becomes the receiver.** The feedback message allows the sender to access whether the receiver has understood the message and the message has had the desired impact. In case of doubt by the receiver, s/he may ask for further clarification of some part of the original message. Even silence is a kind of feedback as certain message does get conveyed in the process.

There are of course exceptions, the communication process does not allow for feedback in the case of one-way communication, for example in the case of memos, newsletters, and announcements, in such cases there is always a risk of the intended message not being understood by the receiver. In the workplace, managers may have difficulty in accessing the effectiveness of their communication in the absence of a feedback.

1.3 Types of Communication

Pre-reading Activity
Is it necessary for communication to be face-to-face always?
How is written communication different from oral communication?
How do people who cannot speak communicate?

Now, think about this- A communicator has several options available when s/he encodes the message that is to be transferred to the receiver. This encoding process is also dependent on the skills of the sender in a particular medium and on the cultural environment where the communication process is taking place. Any message must necessarily have a medium. The medium is like air which is needed for transmission of sound from one place to another.

When we are encoding, the medium gets selected almost spontaneously based on purpose and circumstances. The medium may be using words, be it written or oral; or it may be using body language, signs, and other media that either does not or does have limited use of words. If the message is sent through words, then it is called **verbal communication** and if the sender is communicating through using other media, then it is called **non-verbal communication**. There are many factors which affect the relationship between the sender and the receiver. Therefore, communication, be it verbal or nonverbal, they both are products of social, cultural, and educational environments within which a sender and the receiver participates in a communicative process. This is how the medium acquires the meaningfulness of the message and the message becomes mutually intelligible. If there are no common reference points, be it language or gestures, the sender and the receiver will not understand one another. Therefore, both the participants should be familiar with the codes being used to transfer the message.

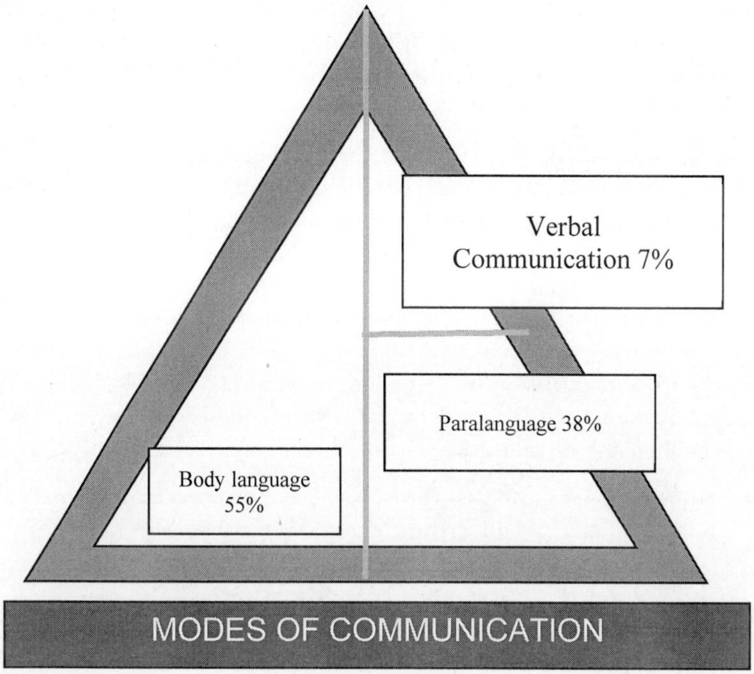

Fig. 1.1

There are further sub-divisions of verbal and non-verbal communication.

Media of communication

1. Verbal
   Oral
   Written
2. Nonverbal

Sign language (audio-visual)
Body language
Paralanguage
Proxemics
Chronemics
Haptics
Listening
Silence

1.3.1 Verbal Communication

Verbal communication is the most widely used form of communication. It is done by using structured language that operates by using words with established rules of grammar and syntax. Verbal language systems are sophisticated in their ability to convey complicated ideas and are by far the most advanced in terms of their vast vocabularies and range of usage.

Verbal communication is the foremost faculty that separates humankind from the rest of the animal world. Let us understand this through an example- we all know that the first noise that a child makes at birth is by crying. As the child grows, the process of language acquisition continues whereby the exposure of the child to socio-cultural and the educational environment shapes the skills and range of verbal communication. Similarly, language systems have developed over thousands of years and their use is indispensable in our daily lives. The use of words to exchange ideas permits us to encode and decode in a way that provides a degree of definiteness in what we say. Of course, one cannot deny the transmission losses that are bound to occur, but even then, the verbal message has a greater chance of reliability.

Depending on the way we use words to speak or write, verbal communication is further subdivided into **oral** and **written**. Let us discuss them separately.

1.3.1.1 Oral Communication

Have you ever thought about the amount of time that we spend on phone calls daily. Now compare it with the number of letters or emails that you write during the same period. You know now why oral communication is the most basic, popular, and preferred mode of communication. We all indulge in oral communication to satisfy the needs of our day-to-day life. Since we know how important and basic this medium is let us try and understand what are the **advantages of oral communication.**

Advantages of Oral Communication

- **Spontaneous and Immediate** It is spontaneous and hence, the message is encoded and decoded immediately.

- **Speed** It has greater speed since the message needs to be decoded almost as soon as the encoding has occurred. Oral messages have the quality of **instantaneousness** and **simultaneity**.
- **Immediate Feedback and Clarification** Since the receiver is present, the feedback and the need for clarification can be met easily and quickly. As a matter of fact, oral communication has a greater number of cycles per communicative event as the messages and their feedback flow back and forth between the receiver and the sender.
- Oral messages are also **persuasive** in nature as it allows you to use body language and paralanguage simultaneously with oral inputs. This way you can be more persuasive. Think about marketing personnel, medical representatives and yes, lawyers too. You will find they use this skill in their jobs.
- There is a scope for **emphasis, change in the tone, elaboration** etc., even midway through the communication as the sender has the advantage of reading the response of the audience. The possibility of midway correction makes oral communication far more responsive to the receiver's needs.
- It is **economical** both in terms of time and money.
- It has a social function too. It allows a group of people to interact and develop themselves socially.
- It is **less formal** and **less rigid**, so it allows you to be more casual and informal.

Disadvantages of Oral Communication

- It **cannot be documented for future use**: It is ephemeral, that is the moment it is said, it is lost forever. It cannot be documented for future reference.
- The spontaneity can also be a disadvantage as there is **limited time period** for formulation of ideas while encoding and decoding. Hurried planning may lead to confused and logically inconsistent messages.
- Oral messages are to a great extent dependent on the part of the receiver. If the receiver is not attentive the message is lost.
- **Digressions** consume a lot more time with delayed or no result.
- Memory plays a great role in retention of the heard messages. **Forgetting** can be a great obstacle for oral communication.
- In a formal setting, responsibility cannot be fixed in the absence of written records, so the **accountability suffers**.
- **Distortion** of the original message can also take place, since the listener may not remember the details of the logical sequence and the emphasis that the oral message may have intended. Additionally, since there are no records, the message cannot be referred to again, making cross-checking difficult. The grapevine phenomenon is often an outcome of this deficiency.
- One of the biggest disadvantages of the oral medium is that it has no legal validity. In the absence of records, the law does not entertain oral messages as admissible legal evidence.

Despite its disadvantages, the very basic human need to interact and communicate with each other is met through the oral medium. Thanks to developments in technology, the power of oral communication has been further enhanced with the steady progress in the telecommunication.

To enhance the effectiveness of oral communication, it is useful to keep in mind the following:

- **Clarity**
- **Conciseness**
- **Completeness**
  These three features help the receiver understand the meaning and importance of the message without seeking further clarification.
- **Good and apt vocabulary** Choosing the apt word to express yourself helps to maintain the spontaneity and fluency in the language. And the use of right phrases, illustrations and idiomatic expressions help in removing ambiguities too.
- **Appropriate paralanguage** It helps in the effective use of the oral medium. Our voice, tone, pronunciation etc., provide the receiver with the complete expression of our message.
- **The body language and oral message must complement each other** Here, the attention should be paid on the congruity between the oral message and the body language so that the credibility of the overall message does not suffer. Therefore, the oral message must be reflected in the body language of the sender, otherwise, it will lead to ambiguities.
- **An expression of commitment** A good speaker must reflect a quality of confidence and that s/he is committed to what is being said.
- **Good listener** The act of speaking and listening are complementary to each other, so paying attention to what is being said will also allow us to understand the message in a better way.

1.3.1.2 Written Communication

Can you imagine a world without a writing system- no written documents- no written communication- no receipts- no signatures! No, we just cannot!

The modern civilization cannot function without written form. At the outset it should be remembered that written communication is not the same as oral communication written down. Written communication has its own dynamics, but the importance lies in its great ability to organize our knowledge and document it for future reference.

Written communication has become an essential part of our daily lives. Be it school, or buying provisions from the local grocery, getting a piece of land registered in your name, government offices, public transport and what not- they all require written documents in some form or the other. This is why written communication is an important part of business organizations too. In fact, it is impossible to visualize an organisation that does not depend on its use. It allows the system to run efficiently and effectively.

All organisation functions on rules, codes, and conventions, and they are followed for the sake of uniformity across the organisation. These are very often codified and organizational procedures are formulated for the efficient functioning of a system. Written communication helps in formalizing the structure and procedure of its functioning. In the absence of written documentation, we would have chaotic conditions with no accountability whatsoever, making the system dysfunctional. Therefore, the advantages of written communication are:

- It is a creative process, as one has much greater time for encoding the message. The sender can focus adequately on the form and expression. Besides, it allows you to go back and forth over the text, edit, make corrections and alterations to make the message complete, concise, and clear.
- It aids memory as well. A message may often need to include details or long explanations. In such cases, we have the opportunity of going over something repeatedly if it is in written form.
- Since written messages are more coherent and organized, they acquire greater credibility and accuracy. Since it is permanent in nature, the data is verifiable and accurate.
- One of the biggest advantages that a written document offers is the possibility of a future reference. All important matters are therefore recorded in writing so that it can be referred to in future.
- Since documents can be put on record easily, legal validity of the same increases. This is a major advantage over oral communication, policy statements, contracts, orders, accounts- they all exist in written form to help the organisation function in a legal framework.
- In matters of organisation of information, research and study, written communication plays a crucial role. It provides an analytical approach to complex formulations and allows us to incorporate additional and supplementary data.
- It helps an organisation to practice uniformity of procedure even if it spread across a large geographical area. Any policy document or written instructions can be sent across to all the branches of the organisation to ensure uniform practices.
- In the era of the Internet, written communication has a wider outreach since they can project ideas across a larger territory in no time. Just think how an email or an advertisement in the print media, newspaper, or information brochures are useful to cater to our daily needs and how quickly we can access them.
- Since written records can be referred to in future, it helps in assigning responsibility and promotes accountability.

It may however be pertinent to remember that often written communication does not work alone, and visual images and graphical representations are added to increase the impact of the message. Here, we should not forget the role of reading, since this is a complementary part of decoding the message. The complete comprehension of message also depends on the reading skills of the receiver, and this would determine the success of the message transfer. *What listening is to oral communication, reading is to written communication.*

Let us also understand some of the disadvantages of the written communication. They are:

- Written communication can often be uneconomical, both in terms of time and money. The entire exercise of drafting a written document is time consuming and expensive.
- It is often difficult to maintain a record of papers and files.
- Feedback is slower and may sometimes be missing altogether and seeking clarifications is also a slow and time-consuming process.
- Written communication is a literate skill, that is a person needs to be literate. This is what makes this medium restrictive.
- Since written communication is a formal document, it does not help in building interpersonal relationships in an organisation.
- Written communication produces record, and these run the risk of leaking out inadvertently or deliberately too.

Written communication helps the organisation to manage its functions better. To make it more effective, skills in language use, vocabulary, writing style and coherent organisation of information are necessary. A few tips are mentioned here.

The language of the written communication should be direct, precise, simple, and unambiguous. While idioms of a language be appropriately used, one must avoid cliché and hackneyed phrases.

1. One must pay attention to the choice of words. General and everyday common words should be used.
2. Sentences should be short and simple and must not be overloaded with too much content. They should be used in such a manner that they become logical units of the entire message.
3. The writing style should be straightforward and to the point. Complex sentences, phrases, jargon and superfluous description unnecessarily complicate the message and yet transmit no useful additional information.
4. As written communication can be referred to several times and has a long shelf life, one must pay attention while drafting it. Editing and rewriting may become necessary so that the message retains its essential qualities of precision, clarity, and logical unity.
5. Basic rules of grammar should be followed and acceptable and polite language be used. This will not only help in building an effective public relation but also help the receiver understand the message better across time, culture and terrain.

1.3.2 Nonverbal Communication

Communication can also be without words. In fact, according to some studies, only seven percent of all communication is verbal- oral and written taken together. Over 50% is body language, while 38% is paralanguage

Nonverbal communication is often used independently but is usually seen to operate alongside verbal communication. As nonverbal media is not based on complex language systems, they are expressed through physical expression. Also, the cultural environment in which the communication occurs has a prominent role to play. The meanings of nonverbal messages are often approximations and cannot be relied upon completely. Sometimes nonverbal medium is deliberately used but it often emerges as spontaneous phenomenon. Expressions of feelings and emotion is one significant area where nonverbal medium plays an important role.

1.3.2.1 Sign language

Sign language uses symbols that are commonly understood within a particular communicative group. Conventionally, signs derive their meaning by working as substitutes for the idea or thing that they replace. Have you seen a patch of uniform black and white painted bands on the road? These are called zebra crossings, the lane that pedestrians use to cross the road. This is also a kind of sign.

Signs are abstractions, and people must agree on the meaning of signs for them to work. Usually, they can convey simple messages because it is not possible to express complex ideas with symbols of limited scope. Road signs, traffic signs, graphs, maps, alarm, sirens- all convey their respective messages. Sign language is audio or visual, depending on the receiver's sensory faculty that is being addressed by the sign. A combination of the two, that is the audio-visual, has become a unique medium of communication.

Audio signs are sounds that convey messages addressed to our faculty of hearing. It is one of the most ancient communication practices, as that imitates wild animals and their method of communicating. Drumbeats and conch blowing have been variously used to warn of danger. Despite its primitive connections, sound signals continue to be used, particularly for purposes where immediacy is required, and visual signals cannot be seen. Ambulance hooters, fire tender sirens- they all fall in the category of audio signs. In the workplace sound signals are used as markers of time periods, like the siren in factories, announcing shift change, alarm clock, office buzzer, the doorbell, telephone ring and the car horn are all example of audio signs. The advantage is that it is a fast medium that can spread to many receivers who may be scattered over a large area.

1.3.2.2 Visual signs

Visual signs are basically graphics and illustrations that have some associative meaning in their design. The picture of a child running with a school bag on a road suggests that there is a school ahead on that road and one needs to slow down. Similarly, the picture of a plate, a spoon and a fork suggest that there is a restaurant ahead where a traveler can have some refreshments.

The main advantage of visual signs is that they can condense a message so that the receiver can grasp the meaning at one glance. This is one of the primary reasons why highway road signs use the visual sign language. They also have a universal appeal and do not disadvantage people who are unfamiliar with a particular language. Certain signs are understood the worldwide like the meanings of traffic lights- red, orange, and green. Besides visual signs are like maps and graphs which serve to illustrate and enliven the contents rendered in verbal medium. However, it should be noted that the visual signs often combine with written medium for maximum communicability.

1.3.2.3 Audio-visual signs

It is perhaps the most popular medium of communication in the modern times. Mass media that is television, films, multimedia and social media have become a symbol of modern civilization. Its business potential is immense and as a communicative device, its persuasiveness is unparalleled. From advertising, marketing, interactive websites, it has now been hugely tapped for its immense potential in the modern-day job market.

1.3.2.4 Kinesics- body language

Body language is the most widely used communication medium, yet we seem to attach so little importance to it as most of the messages that are sent out by our bodies are involuntary. The body constantly sends signals to receivers even when we do not intend it. So long as there are people watching us, our body language continuously transfers messages. This is to an extent a reflex action where our body does not wait for a conscious mind to signal messages.

But what are these messages and how are they understood.

Let us understand in this way- the movement of different parts of our body convey body language. The sender and the receiver understand the meaning of these movements in a particular cultural environment that they share. Here it must be understood that the body movements are often determined by internal psychological stimuli like emotions, feelings etc., emotions like anger, restlessness, joy, sadness, or dejection find expression more by body language than by its verbal counterpart. In this respect body language is a good gauge to measure the psychological disposition of a person. However, body language is indicative and cannot be relied upon fully, since there may be gross misunderstandings of gestures. Even then it is useful because it informs the receiver about the state of the sender's mind in advance.

Body language can also be mastered through training and practice as actors and dancers do in their performance. But most people use body language quite spontaneously without being too conscious of the fact that they are using it. Let us look at some of the important body parts that we use to communicate.

1. **Head and face**

The head has an important role in communicating body language. It is positioned at the apex of the body and hence it is the most visible part. The head seats all the senses, while the face displays them- together they constitute an important and useful means for transmitting and receiving messages.

Just pay attention and recall what does movement of the head signify- it signifies affirmation and negation. The face is a significant part in kinesics. The emotional disposition of a person often shows up in facial expressions. Feelings like embarrassment, surprise, anger, boredom, disgust, fear, and happiness show up on the face unconsciously.

2. **Eyes and eye contact**

Perh2aps the most expressive part of the face, the eyes not only receive signals but also provides an important focus for face-to-face communication. Proper eye contact is required when two people interact. A person who maintains a proper eye contact is understood to be sincere and committed and on the other hand a wandering gaze often suggests distraction, inattentiveness, guilt, or impatience. However, it must be remembered that proper maintenance of eye contact is also a cultural phenomenon, and its interpretations may vary across cultures.

3. **Gestures**

Gestures convey meanings by movement of limbs. It helps to add emphasis to oral communication. They are often involuntary and sometimes habitual too. The human body has a visual appeal and uses this to its advantage in communication. When the receiver is at an inaudible but a visual distance, a person may use gestures to communicate like waving the hand to say 'bye' or showing the full palm to say 'stop.' Again, it is emphasized here that gestures are conventional, and its meaning is embedded in the culture. Receivers understand a gesture by their prior exposure to a particular code.

One must also understand that too many gestures may be counterproductive. It tends to distract focus and unnecessarily dramatizes the spoken word. Since the interpretation of gesture is highly culture specific, one must keep in mind that a wrong gesture can be hilarious, annoying, undesirable, and unpleasant.

If the gestures and the words spoken alongside do not complement each other, the overall message would be neither persuasive nor convincing. Gestures can be learnt and may go a long way in training a person to use them very effectively for business purposes. *What illustrations are to written text, gestures are to speech.*

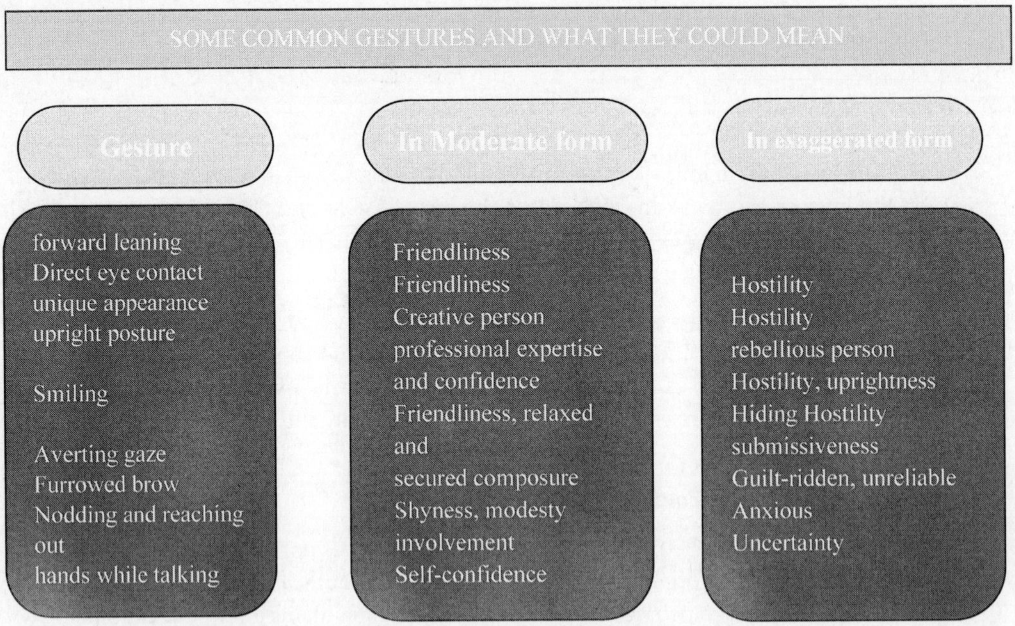

Fig. 1.2

4. Posture

It is technically defined as the way your backbone holds up the body and again like gestures this too is involuntary. As a matter of habit formation, posture is perhaps the first thing which is noticed in a person. The overall positioning of the body certainly conveys the very first impression. Posture also suggests personality traits. An erect posture would suggest self-confidence as much as a slouching one would signify sullenness.

5. Appearance

Now after posture, appearance is then overall view of the body that is presented before the viewer or the receiver. It is a combination of body shape, movement, gesture, and posture- that the person presents. It can be involuntary or voluntary. The outward representation of the self is enhanced further by the way one dresses up or grooms. It is important to remember the occasion for which one is dressing up so that one is congruent with the event and does not attract unnecessary attention. Often, culture determines these choices. For example, black clothes are worn in western funeral whereas white and light-colored clothes are worn in Indian funerals.

When we talk about the workplace, appearance has an impact on the way a person discharges his responsibilities. The way a scientist dresses is more often very different from a manager working in a multinational company.

1.3.2.5 Paralanguage

Paralanguage is the meaning conveyed by **'how something is said.'** Oral communication is **'what is said.'** The occurrence of **how** and **what** distinguishes the two from one another. Therefore, it is impossible to have paralanguage without oral communication. Paralanguage is one of the most powerful complementing media that oral communication possesses over written. How a particular message is said determines its measure of importance to a great extent. To see what role they play in the nonverbal medium let us take up some of the paralinguistic feature and learn about them.

Imagine what happens when a phone rings- a **voice** says HELLO, what are the first few things we learn about the caller apart from the meaning of the five-letter word HELLO? You will be surprised by how much you can learn from the paralanguage of the message.

First, you will be able to make out the gender of the caller; second whether it is an identifiable or a familiar voice; third, if the voice is unfamiliar, fourth, from the way the word is spoken you may be able to assume the socio linguistic or educational background of the person. Now stop and think- none of these meanings are contained in the word HELLO.

These interpretations are all derived from the paralinguistic features of the word HELLO and not the oral communication itself. Therefore, we can say that paralanguage helps to add further meaning to the oral communication.

Likewise, you will find that **volume variation** and **pitch variation** also play an important part in further interpretation of a message. You must have noticed that **volume variation** makes oral communication lively where the voice may fall to a whisper to share some secret or roar and yell to indicate anger. Similarly, **pitch variation** allows an oral message to acquire dynamism. It helps to remove the monotony of the speech and make the articulation persuasive.

Speed and taking **pause** during speaking also communicates or add up to a paralinguistic interpretation of speech. If a person is in a hurry, he/she rushes through the words without waiting to see if the receiver has understood it. Pauses are taken to provide the receiver with certain gaps to interpret the message. But too many pauses is taken at inappropriate place may cause distractions and impatience in the receiver. On the other hand, well-timed pauses help the listener in becoming more attentive.

Word stress is another important dimension of paralanguage. Word stress could be of two kinds when words are stressed in a sentence and when different syllables in a word get stressed to bring about subtle changes in the meaning.

For example, when **word stress works in a sentence:**

Is this how you ***play****?*

Is this how ***you*** *play?*

Is this ***how*** *you play?*

Is ***this*** *how you play?*

Notice that the shift in stress in words of same statement makes the emphasis change. The second level of word stress is that of **stressing syllables in a word** to indicate how they are used in a sentence.

Pre*tend (Noun)*

*Pre****tend*** *(Verb)*

Ex*hibit (Noun)*

*Ex****hibit*** *(Verb)*

The syllables are stressed differently to convey the different meanings. Therefore, one must make the effort in learning the appropriate stresses while pronouncing words as it can also bring about a change in the meaning of the sentence.

1.4 Channels of communication

Pre-reading activity

- Have you ever thought why it is easier to communicate with your friends than your teachers? Why do we prefer to tell or confide something in our friends or siblings than our parents. Some of us also live in joint families and we find ourselves closer to a particular member/s in that set-up, perhaps our grandparents than others. But do you think you can communicate everything to your grandparents?
- Let us talk about an organisation, how to do think the information is communicated in an organisation. Do you think the cycle of communication is complete only when all the participants participate in it. Or, is communication complete when only the boss talks and subordinates listen? How are rumors

and gossip communicated in an organization? Can you draw a similarity between formal organization and family set-ups? Are gossips also part of our personal and social being. Let us explore them in this unit.

Introduction

Channels are paths or routes taken for communication within the organisation. The organisation structure creates a network of paths through which information flows in designated directions. These channels are lifeline for any organisation because they allow it to perform its tasks and functions smoothly. They are categorized into two broad categories: formal and informal.

1.4.1 Formal Organizational Channel

The formal organizational structure clarifies the roles and the relationships between these roles. It charts out functional units, their inter-relationship and delegation of work and authority. These are important determination since the people in the organisation must know whom to communicate with, for what purpose and how. This channel is often referred to as decision-communication network.

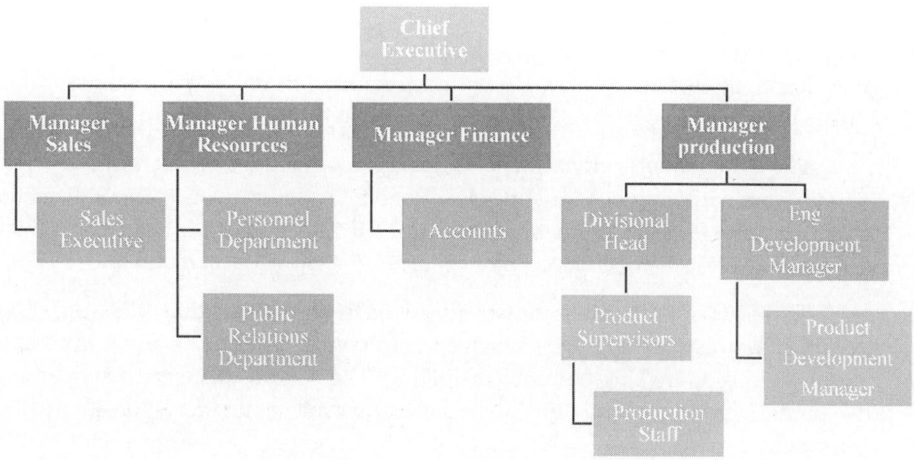

Fig. 1.3 Organisational Chart

1.4.2 Communication Networks

Communication is not simply a matter of individual exchanges between sender and receiver. There is an important social dimension when communication occurs in organizations. This social communication occurs through systems or networks. The larger the size of the organization, the greater is the need for well-structured communication networks.

Unrestricted information may create information overload. People may become selective or simply ignore certain messages. There would be inaccuracies and faulty responses since there is too much of information to process. Organization communication follows certain patterns in the transmission of messages. The most prominent among them are **the wheel, the chain, the circle, and the all-channel network.** *Business English, 2011.*

In the **wheel or the star network**, the individual members communicate with the central member separately. This kind of network may be seen when the central member is a superior authority and surrounding ones her/his subordinates. The wheel network represents centralization of authority, where the center has a great deal of control and coordination in the dissemination of information.

The **chain network** illustrates a situation where two members at the far ends of the chain have to communicate with the central person through their respective intermediaries. It is like a relay race. The intermediaries relay messages to the top. Thus, the two ends may send or receive information after it has been routed through an intermediary/ies and the central person. This network is centralized. However, the intermediaries share with the center the control and authority of the channel. The organizational chain of command is a good example of this network.

The **circle network** has its members situated in a position whereby an individual may communicate with two others next to him. They can communicate along the circular structure and there is no central figure as such. This network has a great degree of egalitarianism and may be often seen in horizontal communication where people at the same level interact with one another.

The **all-channel network** allows maximum freedom where anybody may communicate with just about anyone else. Not only is this network decentralized but it is also a route for fast information exchange. The all-channel is a major contributor towards grapevine channels and could be misused to spread rumors too.

These networks fulfil important functions in an organization. The centralized networks like the wheel and the chain help in receiving information and feedback for informed decision-making or problem solving. The central members play a crucial role in the communication link and, therefore, have a great responsibility and opportunity to exercise leadership, motivate others and pass on selective information. The surrounding members also know the importance of the central figure since information flows through them. The centralized networks are very effective for use by the formal channel.

The decentralized networks like the circle or the all-channel provide for free flow of information. Since these are free of centralized control, they can be creative and may come up with ingenuity and innovation in problem solving. The openness of these networks allows the members to become sociable and participatory in organizational matters. These networks support the grapevine or the formal channel in the organization.

1.4.3 Formal Channel

The formal organizational structure clarifies the roles, relationships delegation of work and authority. These are important determination since the people in the organization must know whom to communicate with, for which purpose, and how. The formal channel is often referred to as the decision-communication network.

The formal channel is the most effective channel because it helps to meet organizational objectives. It runs alongside the hierarchical line of authority where communication is related to the discharge of organizational activities. The formal channel is directly linked to the organization's structure where messages move through defined and planned paths. This is often referred to as 'the proper channel' as communication touches those important points in the structure that have something to do with the message. The formal channel is the authorized communication line of control for the management and as such plays an important role in operational matters. *Business English, 2011.*

1.4.3.1 Advantages

- One of the main advantages of the formal channel is its **effectiveness**, brought about by following the chain of command. Instructions, orders, etc., carry the weight of authority as well as definiteness so that subordinates know for sure what they are supposed to do. Similarly, superiors too receive feedback which enables greater understanding of problems and therefore, more effective decision-making.
- The formal channel can provide more **credible information**, since it originates and is carried forward through designated authority. This also means that information can reach out across even larger organizations with lesser chances of distortion/dilution.
- The 'proper channel' often takes care of information overload by **filtering**. A well-structured organization would delegate functions so that the job is done at its own appropriate level.
- Since people have designated roles in the formal structure, they know their sphere of authority and responsibility. This contributes to establishment of **harmonious environment** in the organisation.
- The formal channel depends on the organizational hierarchy and insists on **accountability**. Information sent through this channel is, therefore, verified authentic and credible.

1.4.3.2 Disadvantages

- The biggest drawback with the formal channel is its very **formality**. There is a certain dryness, absence of warmth and distancing which occurs in the use of this channel. In the attempt to avoid any legal dispute or ambiguity, messages are continuously edited and made to steer clear of these uncertainties.
- The second limitation is the channel's **obstruction of free flow of information**. The formal channel passes through authorized or designated points in the organizational structure. Since there is a great deal of exercise of authority and control, messages do not have the freedom of movement.
- Apart from problems of free flow, the formal channel is a comparatively **slower** channel. Since there could be several intermediaries in the travel path of a message, the transfer becomes a slow process.
- Insistence of formality, proper procedure, or technical requirements- being over-formal may negatively affect the main function of an organization, by giving greater prominence to **procedure over purpose**.
- The formal channel is also **expensive in financial terms**. Expenditure incurred on formal channel is largely because of maintenance and documentation of written records that makes the formal channel expensive.

1.4.4 Informal Channel

The informal channel touches all corners of an organization in a non-hierarchical manner and may or may not have relationships with the organizational work. It is more popularly known as 'grapevine.' It is also called rumors and are based on hearsay which cannot be verified. The grapevine channel is driven more by personal need to communicate rather than positional. It has a direct relationship to how people bond with each other in the organization, irrespective of the positions they hold in it. It is oral, undocumented and conveys information that is often based on personal impressions. *Business English, 2011.*

The grapevine channel is common to all organizations as it fulfils a very basic human need: to share and to relate. Human beings are social by nature and, out of this natural compulsion, they are bound to come together to share their thoughts and opinion. Broadly speaking, the grapevine is a social phenomenon that provides not only a sense of freedom from a regimented organizational procedure, but also allows individuals to have the psychological satisfaction of expressing themselves to one another.

For a long time, the grapevine had negative connotation. It was felt that this informal channel had potential to harm as it could spread rumors or false information. The emphasis was on the control of the informal channel. Some of the reasons identified for the spread of grapevine that may harm the organization are:

1. **Insecurity or job uncertainty** prompts individuals to speculate, particularly if the organization is going through a rough patch.
2. **Lack of self-confidence** or the feeling of inadequacy occurs when the status quo in the workplace is altered. For example, when new technologies are introduced, individuals feel that they would be incapable of handling them. This triggers a sense of being redundant and creates misgivings about change.
3. **Formation of a coterie** by the manager may create heartburn among the other members. The people who are outside the 'chosen few' develop a feeling of animosity towards the other, which gets reflected in their informal observations, rumour mongering.
4. The **absence of authentic information** from the management may also fuel the grapevine as people have no alternative but to go by whatever information is available from the informal channel. If the channels of correct information are kept open and the relationship with the workforce is one of trust, the grapevine does not create a crisis for the organization.

Over the last few decades, the grapevine is being considered as an effective tool for organizational communication, from being a potentially risky channel, it is now considered useful by managers. Effective use of grapevine could be done in the following manner:

- Managers should provide **open access** to information so that facts are available to everybody, and they do not need to depend on inauthentic grapevine.
- **Better working environment** based on trust removes misgivings and helps arrest workplace tension and sense of insecurity. This helps in removing the psychological urge to spread rumours.
- Scope for **healthy interaction** among employees through group activities helps create harmony. An organization could provide time slots as part of their work schedule where employees may interact with one another.
- An **open-door policy** may be useful so that any employee can approach the manager for correct information.
- The notice board, newsletters, circulars, etc., could be effectively used to **disseminate information** across the organization.
- **Upgrading skills of employees** and keeping them up to date with new technology helps in instilling self-confidence and self-worth.
- **Participatory decision-making process** creates a sense of being integral to the decision taken or the job to be done. Teamwork helps in keeping the communication channels transparent.
- Managers should **not try to banish the grapevine** (it is next to impossible), rather, work with it. However, if they come across cases where rumours are being spread with malicious intent, they should arrest its spread immediately.

- Maintaining a **culture of transparency** in the organizational structure goes a long way in ensuring that the grapevine is used in a positive way. *Business English 2011.*

Difference between Formal and Informal Channel

Aspect	Formal Channel	Informal Channel
Description	Clearly defines roles, relationships, and delegation of work and authority.	Spreads throughout the organization in a non-hierarchical manner, often known as the grapevine.
Communication Style	Formal and follows specific paths within the organizational structure.	Informal, oral, and undocumented.
Nature of Information	Typically involves official, verified, and credible information.	Often based on rumors, hearsay, and personal impressions.
Purpose	Directly linked to the organization's structure and supports operational matters.	Fulfills the basic human need for sharing and relating but can potentially spread false information.
Advantages	Effectiveness in meeting organizational objectives, credible information, clarity of roles and responsibilities.	Provides a sense of freedom from regimented procedures, psychological satisfaction, and promotes healthy interaction among employees.
Disadvantages	Can be too formal, obstructs free flow of information, comparatively slower, and expensive.	Potential to spread rumors or false information, may lead to insecurity or misgivings among employees.
Perception	Seen as an authorized communication line of control for management.	Once viewed as potentially risky but now considered valuable for organizational communication.
Management Approach	Often emphasizes formality, procedure, and accountability.	Encourages open access to information, trust-building, and transparency.

Table 1.1 (*Business English, 2011.*)

1.5 Cultural Components of Communication

Pre-Reading Activity

The one activity we are constantly engaged in is communication. Despite being one of the most common social activities, communication is said to be complete or successful when the message conveyed is close to the message received. But this is not a mechanized task, as all communications go through certain stages and the interpretation depends on the filters or perceptions of the people involved in the process. These perceptions or filters might vary across cultures. In the context of globalization, we can see the world contracting like never before. More and more people are crossing boundaries of nations, cultures and even languages for the purposes of work, business, cultural or social exchange, or for just pleasure. The diversity of opportunities thus created is turning the limelight on intercultural communication.

Introduction

In this chapter, you will be introduced to the importance of communicating across cultures and how our cultural parameters and conventions influence the way we communicate. We will also discuss in brief about corporate culture which defines the values upheld by an organization.

The next part of the chapter moves from this generalized view to a closer look at cultural variables and how these variables affect business practices. Cultural variables are various aspects of nonverbal communication such as body language, eye contact, commonly misinterpreted gestures as also perceptions of interpersonal space. Religion, notions of time and interpersonal space and gender equality also influence the ways in which we deal with people or conduct our business communication.

1.5.1 Significance of Culture in Technical Communication

The workplace has changed dramatically in the last two decades. Globalization brought people from different parts of the world with different skills together. This global dimension to business has brought about a multiculturally diverse workforce, catering to multicultural societies. People working together can be diverse in terms of race, culture, language, religion, gender, and nationality. So, handling diversity at the workplace becomes an important factor in successful business. The challenge of communicating across cultures-even through a shared language can hardly be overemphasized. After reading this unit, you will be able to understand the significance of culture in communication and develop skills to handle any situation appropriately.

Communication is a dynamic process which takes place verbally and nonverbally. We generally tend to believe that communication largely depends on the words used to convey the message. In addition to it, our social behavior, gestures, tone, body language, all play a very important role in communication. It is this social behavior of a person which speaks volumes to the person receiving the message. This social behavior is learnt from culture. Sensitivity to differences in cultural values can help us reach a common ground with ease and build trust which leads to a successful communication. Thus, culture plays a very significant role in communication.

1.5.2 What is Culture?

The word **'culture'** can have different meanings for different people. The meaning will change completely when we talk about literature, linguistics, anthropology, or science.

The Oxford English Dictionary defines ***culture*** *as evidence of intellectual development of arts, science, etc., in human society and the state of intellectual development among a people culture can, therefore, be understood as the system of shared beliefs, ideas, customs, a common pattern of behavior of a group of people. Culture can be of many kinds-social culture, corporate culture, religious culture, ethnic culture.*

It is culture which gives us the framework of our individual and collective behavior. It helps us to form a perception of the world around us. The way we dress, the food we eat, our kinship or family values, our ideas of ethics and morality are all governed by culture. This also becomes a benchmark for appropriate behavior for all members of a particular community society or nationality. Usually, these unwritten rules are passed on tacitly from generation to generation. *Business English, 2011.*

Similarly, ***corporate culture*** can also be defined. *It is 'the specific collection of attitudes, experiences, beliefs and values mutually agreed upon and shared by the members of an organization'. It lays out the norms and policies followed by employees and the stakeholders of an organization.*

Thus, corporate culture affects leadership styles, personnel issues, professional advancement, employee morale, work conditions, support, work-leisure balance and, most importantly, ease and frequency of intern communication.

1.5.3 Cultures Outside Our Own

Born and brought up in India, how are you expected to know the preferences of Americans, Arabs, Europeans or Japanese? How do the Japanese welcome their guests? Does response to a stranger vary from culture to culture? Will a customer's complaint be treated differently across the globe? For example, in India, prompt replacement of a malfunctioning product might come as a pleasant surprise, while a quick redressal of a complaint in the US is such a conventional business practice, that it is almost taken for granted. It is interesting to note that without necessarily having experienced the world outside most of us have at least some ideas about people from other cultures and background. The Internet has brought the world very closer to us. One is no longer isolated even when one is alone.

Cultural sensitivity helps you to see the diversities and variations not as potential areas of conflicts, but as a resource to reach out and connect. Societies and people across the world function on certain premises of basic human and social values. For successful intercultural communication, one needs to acknowledge and accept these differences in conventions and value systems and view them from the right perspective. You will learn more about the impact of cultural variables at the workplace in this section.

1.5.4 Communicating Across Cultures

Language can also pose a challenge in intercultural communications. In India, bilingualism/multilingualism is a common feature, so communication is not really hampered. However, at times even a common language may become a barrier if the communicators/ interlocutors come from different backgrounds. The accent or pronunciation might be different. Language can be acquired by anyone who is willing to learn. It is the nonverbal culturally specific traits which cannot be acquired. It is said that even before learning to speak, a child learns the intonation of the language first. Hence, it is seen that even while speaking a common/dominant/second language, the intonation pattern of the first language is evident. It is not possible to completely give-up the influence/ interference of the first language and learn the intonation of the second. It is true that language acquisition can give you knowledge of the culture, and it can be an effective tool in cross-cultural communications, but it cannot automatically transfer the value systems or perceptions of the new culture. Awareness and sensitivity to the cultural variables will go a long way in paving smooth communication channels and establishing good professional and social relationships.

1.5.5 Cultural Variables

Now you are familiar with the word culture. You know that it is socially learned behavior which is extremely diverse across the world. **Many subcultures can be a part of a dominant culture. Subculture is the slight variation in cultural practices and is followed by a smaller group or community within the larger group.** Thus, all humans might carry out the same tasks, but in different ways because they belong to different cultures. The social and cultural variations in the way we talk, eat, dress, and conduct ourselves are evident in our everyday behavior. These culture-specific cues are called cultural variables.

Have you noticed how children imitate their elders? They can tell us how culture is passed on from generation to generation. Children are guided by their families and the community or the culture group they belong to- but they cannot be kept away from outside influences too. In multicultural societies, keeping close to the roots of one's tradition can become a challenging task. In today's world people develop multiple identities and show traits of multiculturalism where an individual is part of both a dominant as well as a local culture. Hence, one might be doing the same social activity, certain gestures or signs can stand out as different or even unique. For the smooth flow of communication across cultures, one needs to understand these different as well as unique expressions of universal human conduct.

1.5.6 Sign Language

Some visual or audio symbols used are universal. For example, traffic and road signs, signs for public utility and public services, which can be easily understood by both literate and non-literate, and across various linguistic groups. In order to reach a wider audience, most of the audio or visual signs do not fall under the category of cultural variables though they are the oldest forms of nonverbal communication. Most of these signs are widely used today. It is the language used in audio-visual signs, especially in the creation of advertisements for circulation through the electronic or print media, that needs to be understood as a cultural variable.

1.5.7 Language Used in Audiovisual Signs

Advertisements communicate messages to an audience within the shortest possible time. India has been a traditionally multilingual country, yet Hindi and English have for a long time maintained their distinct identities. An advertisement space in English would reach a limited English-speaking group and might indirectly be seen to be campaigning for an upmarket/high-end or even a luxury product. The advertisement in Hindi and any Indian language would reach out to the masses, both in cities and villages-all the way to the hinterland. Now the use of language has evolved, the increasing use of Hinglish- a hybrid of English and Hindi, is reflective of the cultural change which has reached our hinterlands too.

1.5.8 Body Language

Fidgeting, sitting cross-legged, or with one foot at a higher level, putting one's arms around the companion's shoulder or waist, all convey nonverbal messages. How these cues are interpreted by the parties involved depends on individual culture and conditioning. Indian culture in the era of globalization and economic liberalization is changing at a fast pace. And yet, these changes are not uniform across the geographical or social parameters of the country. For someone from outside, we are Indians, but for each other, we belong to unmistakably different religious, social, linguistic, and regional groups. The diversity of our land is maintained in the workplace as much as in our personal lives. We show these cultural markers by our dress and food preferences; the sacred thread we might wear around our body or the food we eat at festivals.

Let us look at some features of body language like gestures, use of interpersonal space, eye contact practiced as part of non-verbal communication across the world.

1. **Handshake**

A traditional and widely used form of greeting in the West, it has gained popularity in India too. But it is done differently across the world.

A handshake for:

Spaniards: It must last six to seven strokes less than that is seen as rejection.

Chinese: As people here dislike touching, they might give a weak handshake.

Americans: Firm handshake is acceptable.

Middle Easterners: Gentle, frequently repeated handshakes

French: Light, quick, repeated upon arrival and departure, not offered to superiors.

German: Brusque, firm.

Asians: Gentle, still an unfamiliar mode of greeting for many.

Indians: At the workplace, among English speakers, firm; for others, it is of short duration and is usually not offered to seniors or women in personal relationships, Indian forms of greeting are still preferred across gender and age.

Table 1.2 *(Business English, 2011.)*

2. **Eye contact and Eye Movement**

In America and Britain, maintaining eye contact during formal speeches is acceptable. It denotes honesty and transparency in business dealings. In many Asian countries like Indonesia, Japan, and China, keeping one's eyes lowered is a sign of respect. In India, this rule of not looking into the eyes is especially observed when dealing with seniors and women. Staring in any part of the world is, of course, considered rude. However, a westerner might interpret lowered eyes as a sign of dishonesty or deceit.

3. **Saying Yes/No**

It is one of the most common responses in all communication, and yet surprisingly ways of saying 'yes' or 'no' also vary across cultures. For example, people in Japan move their right hand to say 'no', Americans and Canadians shake their heads back and forth, and people in Bulgaria nod up and down. For most north Indians, moving the head from left to right indicates denial, while moving the head up and down means 'yes'.

4. **Some Commonly Misinterpreted Social Cues**

Sometimes, Filipinos smile and laugh when they are angry. Using the left hand to receive or give money or gifts is considered disrespectful in some Asian cultures as the left hand is considered to be 'unclean/impure'. No such taboo exists in the western cultures. A smiling, nodding face of a Japanese might be perceived as comprehension and acceptance of the message while the gesture indicates that the person is still listening. The popular sign of 'okay' with the thumb and forefinger together might be considered obscene in parts of Italy, and rude and insulting in Germany and Brazil.

1.5.9 Perceptions of Interpersonal Space

For Indians, spatial distance maintained between two people indicates the formality, informality, intimacy, as also the category of relationship. Generally, with seniors, elders, strangers, and members of the opposite sex, one keeps a respectful distance; while with friends and colleagues, the arm's distance rule is relaxed. In fact, it is commonplace to see peer groups walking hand-in-hand or with an arm across the other's shoulders.

Outside India, one will find that Arabs and Latin Americans prefer to stay close during a conversation, while a distance of less than five feet during a business conversation is considered uncomfortable for Canadians and American. People from Japan and Germany prefer their business counterparts to be standing even further away. Clearly, a person who is unaware of this cultural variation might give offence where it was not intended.

1. Social Variables

Social variables divide people into larger groups. People who belong to a particular social group can be identified by the religion they practice, the social norms of dress, food preferences, etc. they follow. These in turn define their worldview, that is, the person's attitude to public and private, kinship value, hierarchy, status, etc. These attitudes go on to influence their business practices, decision-making patterns, concept of time, etc.

2. Religion

In India, as in some areas abroad, almost all homes and commercial establishments have a suitable space reserved for images or symbols of the deity. All believers routinely seek God's blessings-especially before beginning the day, a new project or entering new premises. Some people might publicly follow certain rituals, while others might be more inclined to keep their faith private. Being a multi-religious, multicultural society, Indians are quite familiar with this plurality of belief, and individual faith does not usually interfere with their business or personal relations with fellow-Indians.

3. Food

Food is not only necessary for survival; it forms the most diverse and thriving example of cultural variety. Raw fish might be seen as a delicacy in Japan, while its sight and smell can be repulsive to people from certain parts of the world. Traditionally groups and communities were conservative in their approach- they stuck to the traditional food. While vegetarianism or turning vegan (a vegetarian who abstains from animal and dairy products) might be a fad in the West today, in India it is a way of life for many people. The Indian ethos of spiritualism forbids killing for food. Hence, Indians are famously known to carry their food abroad. Various emigrants, for example, in their desire to maintain their links with tradition and culture, have established little Indias or little Chinas outside their own country. These pockets cater to almost all the cultural needs which help to maintain the parent culture.

4. Dress

The way one dresses reflect one's personality and culture. Traditional forms of dress are easy and immediate identifiers of cultural identity. As with food, dress was once dictated by the climatic, social, and even religious considerations. Nowadays, people are increasingly adopting cosmopolitan modes of dressing because it is seen to be more convenient and allows greater mobility. Yet, ethnic and religious conventions have a certain say in the local dress code. The headscarf or Muslim veil, the Sikh turban, and the Arab headgear are highly visible and culture specific parts of dress. Traditionally acceptable in all cultures, the stress on visible secularism has, however, made these symbols unacceptable in certain parts of the western world.

5. Sense of Public and Private

Indians are known for their warmth, friendly attitude to strangers and almost never seem to be too busy for their family and friends. Indians are seen to be driven more by heart, while western society places greater value on a rational thinking or approach. Also, like other Asians, for people from India, the family and the community usually come before the individual. Our sense of public and private is hence quite diffused and fluid. Our colleagues are welcomed home and family matters might be discussed with colleagues in the office. The western sense of relationships is almost the opposite- the family is private, not to be mixed with the public domain, which is the workplace.

In the West, privacy is treasured, while in Eastern societies, allowing the public and private to intermingle is an accepted social convention. Indeed, the world is seen as one large family. Of course, for both the East and the West, the difference in attitudes have resultant benefits and problems.

6. Time/Punctuality

Differences in perception of time as seen and practiced by different cultures make this issue rather complicated in cross-cultural interactions. Misunderstanding and disappointment are seen as familiar fallouts. **'Time is money'** this value is ingrained in the western culture where time is viewed as a strictly linear, limited resource. Punctuality is fundamental in their lives and anyone who maintains this concept is considered to be a completely professional person. We Indians work and live at our convenient pace. Trains, buses and even bridegrooms are known to be running perpetually behind the schedule.

In cross-cultural context, it is important to be aware of this variation in perception of time to avoid misunderstandings. To an Indian, the desire to stick to the schedule might be seen as impatience, while to a westerner, overshooting of deadlines will be seen as unprofessional. While dealing with westerners, it makes good business sense to take schedules and appointments seriously. Efficiency is a desired virtue in today's globalized world.

Let us now understand the overall impact of the cultural variables on attitudes which affect business. In dealing with multicultural societies or international organizations, awareness of cultural variables can equip you with the required pattern of communication and behavior. By seeing the 'other' in the right or neutral perspective, being alert to culture cues- one can win half the battle in intercultural communications. This helps in the building of confidence in interpersonal relationships, leading to success in business dealings.

Best Intercultural Practices for Organizations

- Follow open door policy.
- Allow direct and indirect flow of communication within the organization.
- Designate a PR as in-house facilitator who can circulate and communicate ideas right across the board.
- Implement recruitment policies which are diversity friendly-across gender, race, community and even for the disabled.
- Widely circulate through notices, posters, slogans the company's core values.
- Managers should be suitably alert towards diversity issues and stereotyping.
- Corporate social responsibility should be practiced in word and deed.

Best Intercultural Practices for Individuals

- Be receptive to people.
- Build a positive outlook in all intercultural communications.
- Avoid discussing religion, personal matters or even politics in intercultural situations.
- Do not interrupt or unduly impose your ideas on the other person.
- Find out about others' culture and try to understand culture cues in the conversational discourse.
- Be aware of culture specific gestures and avoid gestures which might confuse or annoy.
- In intercultural communications, attitude to time, sense of acceptable space, acceptable dress, manners, and notions of hierarchy play a very important role. Be appropriately informed to ensure smooth communication.
- Remember, across all languages and cultures, it pays to be polite.
- Respect all differences and never ridicule other's culture.
- Stay away from stereotypes and prejudices.

- Avoid sexist language or behavior.
- Avoid all discriminatory practices.
- Remember, equal employment and access to opportunities is everyone's right.
- Be honest with yourself and others, you will be respected for it.

1.5.10 Gender Sensitivity

You have already learnt that our social identity is shaped by cultural values and perceptions, and it varies from nation to nation, and region to region. Now we are going to learn about a very important factor that is even more basic to the framing of our identity and that is gender. The norms of behavior, the dress we wear, the preferences we might have, our sense of personal space, are all decided by our gender also. Let us look at how we generally identify women and men and also how we mark gender divisions.

In traditional modes of understanding identity, the roles of mothers, wives, daughters, and sisters firmly place women in the social hierarchy and in various relationships to men, and of course, to each other. Once Simone de Beauvoir said: 'One is not born, but rather becomes a woman'. The truth of this statement is borne out by women in a wide spectrum of human experience. One is born a biological male or female but becomes a man or a woman through an elaborate system of cultural conditioning. How does this form of identity affect the lives of women and men? How and why is it a different human experience? What is the importance of understanding gender?

In this part of the unit, you will look at how people are put into the two categories of male and female, and how subsequent cultural perceptions of men and women affect the workplace.

What does it mean to be a woman? As per the CBSE results of Class X and XII, girls usually outshine boys in academic performance every year almost consistently. So, if job selection depends on merit, why are more men employed than women? It exposes the huge gender gap in world economy, and the denial of certain rights to women. It also speaks of the traditional attitudes towards women. This, in turn, leads to the perception that women are best suited for nurturing roles as they are kind, sensitive, emotional, and caring. Understanding gender will help you to see how men and women are projected, and how society perceives them, or how it wants to perceive them.

1. Understanding Gender

Oxford English Dictionary defines gender as grammatical grouping of words (nouns and pronouns) into classes- masculine, feminine, and neuter- accordingly as they are regarded as male, female or without sex.

A definition which is used commonly in language study- it has larger implications when it is transferred to the extended meaning in society. Gender is not to be confused with biological male or female sex. Gender is to be understood as the social and cultural construction of roles in modern society which are given to the two respective categories of male and female. Gender then determines our behavior, activities, and attributes, that a given society considers appropriate for men and women, respectively. Male and female are biological categories, masculine and feminine are cultural categories. These roles are also hierarchically arranged, where male occupies a higher position than a female in social setting. *Business English, 2011.*

Since gender is the most visible sign of difference it becomes very easy to stereotype. One could say, for example, that men are often stereotyped as being aggressive and risk takers, while women are stereotyped as being docile and cautious in their attitude. When these stereotypes are allowed to enter the workplace, the implications hugely disadvantage the woman. As a result of the feminine stereotype of women being kind, sensitive and emotional, and also passive and lacking in leadership qualities, many women, despite their qualification and caliber, are not picked for top jobs. This popular perception of women being the weaker sex, when combined with the limited social space granted to them, restricts their potential and raise doubts about their capacities.

From boyhood, males are suitably trained and expected to be in complete control of themselves and the situation. To show their manliness, or masculinity, they are consciously exhorted to be not like a woman. This develops the male stereotype of being disengaged, authoritative and rational. Conforming to this stereotype leads to high stress levels in adult lives, as men are denied the safety of expressing their natural emotions. On the other hand, for young girls, notions of feminine beauty and docility might be enhanced at the cost of intellectual development. How do you think people respond to these stereotypes? What about the lone boy who develops a passion for classical dance and is never seen on the sports ground or roughing it out with the other boys? All forms of creative arts are supposed to be feminine activities. In an Indian home, how many mothers are happy with their son's interests in cooking or dress designing, and the daughter's interest in football or in bicycle repair? Do you think a fluid idea of gender space/construction is necessary?

2. Gender Discrimination

Any discrimination practiced on the basis of race, gender, class, caste, or disability is an offence the world over. And yet, it continues to be a sad reality for those who do not belong to or conform to the dominant group.

Thus, power equations have always benefited the majority and disadvantaged the racial, ethnic or gender minority. Such disadvantages can be in the form of denial of basic rights, suppression, exploitation, harassment or even violence. Treating men or women unfairly or with prejudice just because of their gender is termed as gender discrimination. It is caused by internalization of age-old perception of gender roles.

The roots of such discrimination against men and women lie in certain culture and religious practices. Such practices and orthodox beliefs have kept men and more notably women in varying stages of restrictions and oppression. Though women have proved their mettle and have come a long way, it is the mindset and stereotypes which is hampering the progress of men and women even today.

3. How Does Gender Discrimination Work?

Financial discrimination is the most widespread and blatant form of discrimination. In the entertainment industry, for example, leading men are paid much more than women actors. The unorganized sector and even the small-scale sector are quite exploitative of all workers, especially women. For the same job, it is considered acceptable to pay less to the woman than the man. Pay averages show a gender gap across the world.

- Though many companies today implement women-friendly policies such as maternity leave packages and flexitime, women who opt for these benefits might stagnate professionally.
- Top-level management jobs are usually denied to women if they ask for flexible working hours.
- Transfers and relocation also become a significant issue if the woman employee is married and is raising a family.
- Male-dominated management teams and the traditional hierarchical patterns in the work sector also become an impediment to a woman's professional progress.

Despite legal and constitutional safeguards for women, discrimination is still practiced in many forms. These laws address issues of overt forms of discrimination, but it is the subtle form, which is difficult to nail, and is more damaging. Some of them are given below:

- Being the traditional bread winners, men have to be achievers, and this is much a pressure on them as it is on women to remain in the background.
- Ambition is seen as a masculine trait; certain cultures frown upon ambitious women.
- Social and cultural restrictions are also gendered. Both men and women have to comply with restrictions that are the result of social prejudices regarding gender and identity. This greatly hampers professional choices available to both.
- Characteristics which are required for top management or high-profile jobs are conveniently closer to masculine traits or male stereotypes. One needs to be aggressive, assertive, bold, and tough to be able to head corporate and business houses. So, men who do not have these traits are as unlikely as women to get the top job.

Hence, gender discrimination is not only practiced with women but equally with men too.

4. Sexual Harassment

Of all the ways in which discrimination is practiced on account of gender, sexual harassment is the worst because it not only violates the individual's sense of dignity and right to earn a living but is also an assault on the person's sense of self-worth. Such an unfair and derogatory practice is a measure of gross insensitivity towards the victim and should be suitably dealt with.

Such harassment exposes the deepest form of gender prejudice against a colleague or subordinate. It especially reflects the highly stereotyped patriarchal attitudes of male superiority and power over a submissive female. Sexual harassment can also be directed by a woman against a man. Any misuse of power, be it by a woman or a man, is equally objectionable.

Gender bias or discrimination in any form bases itself on the continuity of gender stereotypes. Under the guidelines of the Honorable Supreme Court of India, the National Commission for Women has formulated guidelines on sexual harassment at the workplace, which defines the offence and offers a code of conduct and provides measure of redressal against such practice. It highlights the serious impairment or threat to equality in employment when a man or a woman is subjected to gender specific violence. As per the above-mentioned guidelines, sexual harassment is defined as

... [Any harassment which] includes such unwelcome sexually determined behaviour (whether directly or by implication) as:

a) Physical contact and advances

b) A demand or request for sexual favours

c) Sexually-coloured remarks

d) Showing pornography

e) Any other unwelcome physical, verbal or nonverbal conduct of a sexual nature

.........it is discriminatory for instance when the woman has reasonable grounds to believe that her objection would disadvantage her in connection with her employment or work including recruiting or promotion or when it creates a hostile work environment. Adverse consequences might be experienced if the victim does not consent to the conduct in question or raises any objection thereto.

The guidelines also include preventive steps as well as steps to redress grievances, legal and code of conduct at the workplace, with explanations and other details. India is a signatory to many international conventions, including the United Nations Convention on the Elimination of All Forms of Dis- crimination Against Women (CEDAW), which it ratified in 1993. The principle of gender equality is enshrined in the Indian Constitution (Article 11 and Article 15), which not only grants equality to women but empowers the state and makes it obligatory for it to adopt measures of positive discrimination in favor of women.

In the changed scenario, women are rising up to the challenges, creating a niche for themselves in the professional sector. Now, women are regularly featured in the Fortune and Time list of most influential persons or most influential businesswomen. They have broken stereotypes and are inspiring more and more women to take up careers as businesswomen, professionals, and entrepreneurs. Today, parents are keen to educate their daughters along with their sons.

Globalization and the need to cater to multicultural societies and markets are making companies rethink their recruitment policies. Gender disparity is being seriously addressed by adopting gender-friendly policies. Under the pressures of globalization, companies are striving hard to remain competitive in today's marketplace and providing equal opportunities to men and women is giving them the positive edge. Corporate houses are aware that employing a woman would mean bringing new perspectives, displaying lateral and creative thinking which are the new mantras which lend a competitive advantage to companies in the globalized world.

And yet, professionally, women are still largely a disadvantaged group. Although various gender friendly national and international policies and legislations have been formulated and implemented, the gender gap in employment is still a matter of serious concern.

1.5.11 How to Bridge Gender Gap and Develop Gender Sensitivity

- Gender sensitivity cannot just be a matter of individual understanding.
- Organizations and managements need to be gender sensitive and adopt gender-friendly policies.
- Gender disparity in employment should be routinely monitored and rectified.
- Honor the law of equality in word and spirit.
- What employers and organizations can do?
    i) Bring requisite changes in recruitment policies.
    ii) Check discriminatory practices, be it against men or women.
    iii) Follow diversity in employment.
    iv) Provide gender-friendly benefits like maternity-paternity leave and child-care facilities at the workplace.
    v) Flexibility in work hours, parental leave, equal treatment, and income security for women should be accepted as new demands of a diverse work force- and should be seen as an investment.
    vi) Avoid all sexist language or behavior.
    vii) Encourage male employees also to avail of parental leave and extend family friendly policies to them.

Of course, overnight changes in cultural and behavioral patterns are neither possible nor feasible. Yet, concerted efforts need to be put in place to establish a conducive environment in order to address gender issues. Developing gender sensitivity can help in challenging the patriarchal mindset and give women and men their due as equal citizens in a world.

Unit Summary

- *Communication plays an important role in our daily lives*
- *Communication is a process which has essential components, from encoding the message to decoding it.*

- *The process involves equal comprehension skills from both the sender and the receiver.*
- *Communication is done with the help of a medium.*
- *The main media of communication are verbal and nonverbal.*
- *Verbal communication uses words, which can be expressed in oral or written form.*
- *Nonverbal communication includes sign language, body language and paralanguage.*
- *Sign language can be audio, visual or audio-visual.*
- *Culture is an important aspect of communication.*
- *The concepts of gender discrimination, gender sensitive, gender diversity, sexual harassment etc*

Exercises

Multiple Choice:

1. Communication is defined as:
   a. A one-way process of sending messages.
   b. A process of understanding and sharing meaning.
   c. Only verbal interaction between two people.
   d. The method of using signs and symbols to communicate.

2. Which component of communication involves interpreting and making sense of the message received?
   a. Encoding
   b. Decoding
   c. Sender
   d. Medium

3. A Mentor wants to broadcast a message to all the mentees. Assume there are 12 mentees working under his/her supervision. Of the following medium, which is the economical one to communicate with everyone.
   a. Write an Email by putting everyone in cc and advertise about a conference
   b. Schedule for a Tea/Lunch
   c. Invite all the 12 students to his/her office
   d. Call one person and ask him to float the message among others

4. Which of the following is NOT an advantage of oral communication?
   a. It is spontaneous and immediate.
   b. It provides immediate feedback.
   c. It can be documented for future use.
   d. It is economical in terms of time and money.

5. Which of the following is a correct statement about written communication?
   a. Written communication is always more economical than oral communication.
   b. Written communication cannot be used for legal documentation.
   c. Written communication allows for future reference and accountability.
   d. Written communication is always more effective than non-verbal communication.

6. Which type of non-verbal communication involves the use of physical space in communication?
   a. Kinesics
   b. Proxemics
   c. Chronemics
   d. Paralanguage

7. What are the two broad categories of communication channels within an organization?
   a. Verbal and non-verbal
   b. Hierarchical and non-hierarchical
   c. Formal and informal
   d. Written and oral

8. Which network pattern represents centralization of authority in communication?
    a. Wheel network
    b. Chain network
    c. Circle network
    d. All-channel network

9. Which network pattern allows maximum freedom of communication and is decentralized?
    a. Wheel network
    b. Chain network
    c. Circle network
    d. All-channel network

10. What is the primary advantage of the formal communication channel?
    a. Allows for rapid dissemination of information
    b. Fosters creativity and innovation
    c. Ensures credibility and clarity of information
    d. Encourages informal interactions

Answers: 1-b, 2-b, 3-a, 4-c, 5-c, 6-b, 7-c, 8-a, 9-d, 10-c

Subjective Questions

1. Define communication in your own words.
2. Explain the role of feedback in communication.
3. What is the significance of the medium in communication?
4. How does verbal communication differ from non-verbal communication?
5. What is paralanguage?
6. What are the main advantages of written communication?
7. Differentiate between formal and informal communication channels in organizations.
8. How is the grapevine considered as an effective tool for organizational communication?
9. Describe a scenario where non-verbal communication might be more effective than verbal communication.
10. Discuss the importance of understanding cultural differences in intercultural business deals and transaction.

Know More

- *We are biologically wired to communicate; it is not mere an acquired skill. For example, the mirror neurons in our brains are responsible for empathy. Empathy is a quality which enables one to 'mirror' each other's emotions, and effective communication depends on it.*

- *Nonverbal communication frequently conveys more meaning than verbal communication. According to research, body language and tone of voice account for 55% and 38% of nonverbal signals respectively, that influence communication efficacy, leaving just 7% to be attributed to spoken words.*

- *The Sumerians' use of the cuneiform script marks the beginning of written communication, dating back to around 3400 BCE. This approach laid the groundwork for contemporary communication by facilitating the recording and dissemination of complicated thoughts.*

- *Claude Shannon and Warren Weaver developed the Shannon-Weaver Model in 1948, regarded as one of the first communication models. Originally intended to enhance communication, this model included the idea of "noise" or any disturbance that may skew the information being sent.*

- *Culture has a significant influence on communication. Low-context cultures – like the United States – rely more on overt verbal communication, whereas high-context cultures – like Japan – heavily rely on nonverbal cues and the context of the conversation.*
- *Silence may be a very effective and meaningful communication technique when used to communicate for specific purposes. Certain cultures see silence as having more power than words and utilise it to express disapproval, respect and politeness.*

- *Linguists claim that all modern languages descended from Proto-Indo-European, a common language spoken between 4500 and 2500 BCE. This is the root of many languages, including Hindi, Russian, and English.*

- *The telegraph, a 19th-century invention, facilitated instant global message delivery. It transformed the essence of communication and laid the path for subsequent advancements such as the internet and mobile phones.*

- *Emotions and biases are psychological variables that may seriously impede successful communication. Misunderstandings may arise, for example, when someone's emotional condition affects how they comprehend a message.*
- *Confirming that the message has been comprehended as intended is one of the primary purposes of feedback in communication. Writing comments was sluggish in the past, but thanks to contemporary technology, communication can now be done instantly, increasing its effectiveness and interactivity.*

References and Suggested Readings

Fiske, J. (2010). *Introduction to communication studies.* Routledge.

Holliday, A. (2021). *Intercultural communication: An advanced resource book for students.* Routledge.

Tyagi, K., & Misra, P. (2011). *Basic technical communication.* PHI Learning Pvt. Ltd.

DYNAMIC QR CODING FOR FURTHER READINGS

Communication Cycle

Verbal and Non-verbal Communication

Kinesics

Cultural differences in communication

Communication Channels

Gestures around the world

Gender-sensitive communication

2 Routine Technical Communication

Unit Specifics

Communication is the lifeblood of an organization. In this Unit you will learn about various kinds of challenges and opportunities that an organization faces in its internal and external correspondence. As you read this chapter on correspondence, keep in mind the cultural components of communication you have learned in the previous unit, so that your messages are encoded in a manner that reflects your social and cultural sensitivity and concerns.

Let's start this unit by understanding the importance of communication for the effective functioning of an organization. We will look at the basic distinction between interactive and non-interactive techniques of correspondence. The internal written communication forms in an organization are circulars, notices, memos, and office orders; all of which are examples of downward, non-interactive communication. For all these forms of communication, you will learn about the occasions when such correspondence is undertaken and about the formats that are conventionally followed for writing these messages. We will begin with an understanding of how we plan for a meeting by sending out a notification and agenda; and how minutes are written and, in the process, also learn about the techniques of note taking and summarizing.

Once we have understood the internal communication process of an organization, we will move on to the need for and importance of external correspondence. We will identify the various opportunities for both solicited and unsolicited external correspondence and learn some basic formats we can use to write effective letters.

One of the most important kinds of external communication undertaken by an organization is financial correspondence. The final topic in this unit will also discuss about the employment related correspondence you will need to undertake when you are applying for a job. You will be guided about the best way in which you can write an effective biodata and how you should draft a job application letter.

Apart from this at the end of the unit, a succinct recapitulation of the overall concept is provided in form of a unit summary. Besides, a large number of multiple-choice as well as descriptive type questions are included. A list of references and suggested readings are given in the unit so that one can go through them for practice. It is important to note that for getting more information on various topics of interest some QR codes have been provided for different sections which can be scanned for relevant and supportive knowledge.

Rationale

Since you have already learnt about various facets of communication in Unit 1, let us now understand the need for communication in an organization. As we know any organisation can function properly only if their communication process is smooth and effective. But how to make this process effective? What are different kinds of correspondence organisations do to function effectively? In this unit, we will find how organisations communicate. You will also learn about different kinds and methods of routine and business correspondence.

Pre-requisites

Before reading this unit, the students are advised to revisit the following:

Technical Correspondence: Routine and Business (Class XII)

Basic principles of communication mentioned in Unit-1

Unit Outcomes

After studying this unit, students will be able to:

U2-O1: *Apply correct formats and structures for various types of technical correspondence, including collection letters and financial communications.*

U2-O2: *Draft effective collection letters at different stages: mild reminders, persuasive letters, and last resort letters.*

U2-O3: *Write clear and professional correspondence for banking and insurance requests.*

U2-O4: *Create impactful job application letters and resumes, highlighting skills and achievements.*

U2-O5: *Perform a personal SWOT analysis to assess strengths, weaknesses, interests, and values for job applications.*

Unit-2 Outcomes	EXPECTED MAPPING WITH COURSE OUTCOMES (1- Weak Correlation; 2- Medium correlation; 3- Strong Correlation)					
	CO-1	CO-2	CO-3	CO-4	CO-5	CO-6
U2-O1	2	3	2	1	1	2
U2-O2	1	3	2	1	1	2
U2-O3	1	3	2	1	1	2
U2-O4	2	3	2	2	1	2
U2-O5	2	2	2	2	1	1

2.1 Communication: Need Importance and Techniques

Pre-reading Activity

- What are the points you need to keep in mind while writing to a friend?
- How is writing a letter of complaint different from writing to a friend?
- Do you think that the written words are important in a business organization?

2.1.1 Why Should We Communicate?

Communication is the process by which an organization is coordinated and operated. In an organization, the primary tools of interaction are verbal/oral and written. Communication is of prime importance to be able to do the following:

- Anticipate problems.
- Control and check results and receive feedback.
- Coordinate and connect employees and departments towards a common goal.
- Develop strategies for positive outcomes.
- Forecast organizational objectives and policies.
- Impress all stakeholders with the efficiency and integrity of the company.
- Organize-set behaviour patterns for effective functioning,
- Plan programmes, procedures, budgets, etc.
- Respond to the needs of individuals and the market
- Supervise.

Each of these is of crucial significance if the organization is to be a site of interaction among its employees, all of whom work towards the fulfilment of common objective and target. For this interaction to be meaningful, it is important that we first understand what function is performed by the 'messages that we transmit both internally and externally in an organization. Messages to be effective must don this cap and be concise, audience-centred, and purposeful.

Effective messages must also be planned so that they:

- Are clear, convincing, and accurate.
- Clarify and condense information.
- Describe accurately and clearly what the situation is and what needs be done.
- Discuss alternatives and respond creatively to problems.
- Explain the context in which action/response is required.
- Give facts rather than impressions, by using concrete language.
- Highlight and focus on key issues and concerns.

- Persuade you to change your behaviour/ notions/ impressions.
- Provide practical information.
- State precise responsibilities.

Effective communication provides the focus for the members of the organization through interpersonal interaction. It also determines, develops, and maintains the formal relationships among employees, management, and stakeholders.

Communication skills are therefore vital for effective management. Management is a complex process and the first job done by the management is to fix its organizational objectives and frame appropriate policies for their fulfilment. There also must be a system in place, by which the objectives and policies can be guided, coordinated, and controlled to ensure that the stated targets and goals are met.

When the organization has an effective communication network in place, this in turn will facilitate:

- A clear understanding about roles and responsibilities.
- A sense of belonging and commitment.
- Empowerment of employees with information on developments and activities.
- Enhanced job performance and effectiveness.
- Motivation and a sense of identification with the goals and targets determined by the management.
- Smooth effecting of changes in policies and procedures
- The dissemination of information that will convince employees about the reasons guiding changes and decisions. (*Chaturvedi and Chaturvedi, 2004*)

2.1.2 What is the Importance of Technical Correspondence

Technical correspondence refers to all kinds of written communication used for conducting different types of exchanges and transactions within and outside an organisation.

The important functions performed by technical correspondence are:

- Reference and record of day-to-day administration.
- Legal, documentary evidence to be used in case of conflict and litigation.
- Sales and promotion.
- Promotion of goodwill.

The importance of technical correspondence is evident from the above functions and can be understood in the following manner:

- Every organizational activity involves frequent correspondence between the parties concerned.

- Communication is a valuable instrument for initiating, maintaining, and concluding business transaction and relations.
- Written communication facilitates positive, unambiguous, and interactive communication.

Today's workplace is best with multiple communication challenges, which has made our understanding of the theory and practice of correspondence more crucial.

Some of these communication challenges are:

- The size and spread of organizations that have resulted from and led to the creation of a culturally diverse workforce within global organization.
- The advances in technology which have had a great impact on speed, frequency, and reach of communication.
- The concept of human capital wherein the employees' attitudes, interests and welfare are a vital part of managerial concerns and need to be addressed.
- The need to practise economical means in terms of time, manpower and money.
- The importance of having an environment that is professional and personalized.
- The importance of training in corporate etiquette.
- The need for displaying social responsibility in terms of employment and trade practices.
- Team-based collaborative work in place of the conventional command-and-control management structure.

2.1.3 Interactive and Non-Interactive Techniques of communication/ Correspondence

When we interact, we do so as interdependent equals. We expect a response that is displayed in action and in a written 'code'. that is in the same domain as our message. When we use the word 'non- interactive' in the context of technical correspondence we are implying that the 'feedback' to our message will primarily be consequential, that is, have an impact on the future behaviour or actions of an individual or a group of individuals, to whom the message was transmitted.

Both interactive and non-interactive correspondence are sequential and are used to facilitate

- Conflict resolution
- Coordination
- Information sharing
- Problem solving

Non-interactive correspondence can be defined as that which is internal to organization, is formal and written and follows the chain of operational command and function that characterizes the structure of a particular organisation. When the correspondence is done 'non-interactively we are sending a message that is in response to a particular need in the functioning of the organization. *Business English, 2011.*

Some of the common forms of non-interactive correspondence include memos and office orders that concern individuals, and notices and circulars that are addressed to a group of individuals within the organization.

All four kinds of business correspondence are causative and consequential and demand a response normally in the form of action. Other kinds of non-interactive correspondence include communication related to group decision-making in the organization, when the message is sent in the form of notification, agenda, and minutes. This kind of correspondence primarily performs the function of information. However, it also has a catalytic function as it leads to participation by concerned individuals and keeps all stakeholders informed about decisions and changes in policy and procedures.

Interactive correspondence is carried out between the organization and its customers/buyers/stakeholders. While being formal and written, is also mutual and interdependent since it hopes for a positive written as well as action-oriented feedback in terms of patronage and procurement.

Internal Technical Correspondence

Pre-reading Activity

Imagine that you are planning to set up/upgrade a business

Read below to find out why it is important for you to have an organization chart to manage the problems that come with expansion and success.

Imagine you inherit a traditional provision store from your father. The shop is good enough to cater to the requirements of the local community. Now you want to expand it into a new age departmental store. As time passes and you find customers who like your products, you may need to take on an employee to help to absorb some of the workload. Once you start to employ more and more staff, things can get complicated. What will happen when you find that:

- New employees are struggling to understand their responsibilities as no one can spare the time to show them the ropes.
- Queries do not get resolved because your time and availability are spread thinly, and your employees have not been asked to sort it out.
- Work gets neglected or ignored because there is no one to check quality standards or help train new staff.

- Your employees may argue over the tasks they feel they were not asked to do.

This is the right time to consider creating a business organizational chart to help you organise your business more clearly.

2.2 Internal Technical Communication: Dimensions, Directions and Dynamics

What Is a Business Organization Chart?

An organizational chart clearly identifies a company's characteristics to enable both employees and others to identify the structure of your company. It identifies the number of people working in your company, what your company's principles and aspirations are and its chain of command. *Business English, 2011.*

By clearly outlining an organizational structure you will be identifying:

- Who is responsible for what areas of communication.
- Who is responsible to whom.
- Who to go to when problems or queries arise.
- Why the company exists and what it hopes to achieve.

When you are planning this chart, you might want to keep some of these in mind in addition to the points mentioned above:

- What rules and procedures have been conveyed to each employee about their roles as employees within your shop/company?
- As you now know who in-charge is, you can draw a flowchart to indicate the line of command.
- As you now know what roles each of your employees play, you can place each of them in little boxes and give them a job title, which will complement their contract of employment to define their exact roles.

(Have you ever seen an organisational chart? When you browse through the website of your College/ Institute/ University- you will find a flow chart dictating the organisational hierarchy and responsibilities attached to each post).

Basics in Internal Organizational Communication

Effective communication is the foundation for a functional organization. Many organizations take a deliberate, formal approach to ensure sound communication, by developing a communication plan. The premise on which the concern expressed above is based, is that in organizations, the effectiveness of a communication system depends on the extent to which necessary information (required for decision-making) reaches the concerned person at the right time (when the information is needed).

This network of information supports the overall functioning of management by integrating and coordinating the workforce for achieving organizational objectives. Hence, every organization creates a network for information to pass through its different levels of authority and functional heads and units. The flow of communication follows the structure of the organization. (*Chaturvedi and Chaturvedi 2004*)

Key Principles to Effective Internal Organizational Communication

- Unless the management comprehends and fully supports the premise that organizations must have high degrees of communication, the organization will remain stilted. Too often management learns the need for communication by having to respond to the lack of it.
- Effective internal communication starts with effective skill in communication, including basic skills in listening, speaking, questioning, and sharing feedback. These can be developed with some concerted review and practice. Perhaps the most important outcome from these skills is conveying that you value hearing from others and their hearing from you.
- Sound meeting management skills go a long way towards ensuring effective communication.
- A key ingredient to developing effective communications in organization is each person taking responsibility to ask when they do not understand a message, or to suggest when and how someone could communicate more effectively. *Barnard, 1938.*

Basic Structures/Policies to Support Effective Internal Communication

1. *Downward Communication*

- Ensure every employee receives a copy of the strategic plan, which includes the organization's mission, vision, value statement, strategic goals, and strategies about how those goals will be reached.
- Ensure every employee receives an employee handbook that contains all up-to-date personnel policies.
- Develop a basic set of procedures for how routine tasks are conducted and include them in the standard operating manual.
- Ensure every employee has a copy of their job description and the organization chart.
- Regularly hold meetings, even if there is nothing pressing to report. Have meetings anyway, if only to establish and affirm that things are on course, and that there is no immediate problem.
- Hold full staff meetings every month to report how the organization is doing, its major accomplishments, concerns, announcements etc.

- Ensure all employees receive yearly performance reviews, including their goals for the year, updated job descriptions, accomplishments, need for improvement, and plans to help employees accomplish these improvements. *Barnard, 1938.*

2. ***Upward Communication***

- Ensure all employees give regular status reports to their supervisors. Include a section for what they did last week, will do next week, and any actions/issues to address.
- Ensure all supervisors meet one-on-one at least once a month with their employees to discuss concerns. Even if the meeting is an informal chat, it cultivates an important relationship between supervisor and employee.
- Use management and staff meetings to solicit feedback. Do a round table approach to hear from each person and act on feedback from others.
- Develop a Basic Communications Plan: Whether planning your internal or external communication it helps a great deal to develop a communication plan, either informally or formally. For example, consider:
  a. What key messages do you want to convey?
  b. Who are the key stakeholders (e.g., consider clients, funders, community leaders, service providers, etc.) to whom the key messages need to be conveyed?
  c. What is the best approach to reach each key stakeholder, including who/how should the message be conveyed?
  d. How will you know if you are reaching these stakeholders or not? *Barnard, 1938.*

A common model of internal communication is what is referred to as LSM (Line and Staff Management) model. This is used in large organisations comprising line managers and staff managers. Line managers are responsible for the main activities of the company, such as manufacturing and sales, and staff managers control the support and service areas such as accounting, distribution etc., A network of relations between members in the line (functional) management and staff (support) management is created by means of an effective internal common network.

Broadly, all business communication is geared towards the fulfilment of one or more of the following five types of information needs:

- **Statutory information**- which must be conveyed to all employees such as terms and conditions of service.
- **Regular-work-situation**- information regarding routine policies and procedures.
- **Major policy or operational change information**- which will impact a large number of employees and stakeholders.
- **Information bulletin**- periodic updates about events and happenings.

- **Communication by expectancy-** information about critical changes that must be conveyed before major changes are made or decisions taken so that employees are prepared and expect the change and will adapt to it better. (*Chaturvedi and Chaturvedi, 2004*)

2.3 Circulars and Notices

In this section, we will learn about the need, purpose and drafting of effective circulars and notices.

2.3.1 What are Circulars and Notices?

Taken from the Latin word ***circularis***', that is, a circle, the circular disseminates information in a circle to a wide audience. It is addressed not to an individual, but to many persons, through a written advertisement, directive, or notice, and is intended for mass distribution. A notice is also a form of written communication and is intended for public transmission and response.

Given the multiplicity of dimensions and directions of written correspondence in an organization that you are familiar with by now, we can classify circulars and notices as written correspondence that is:

- Internal
- Non-interactive
- Downward

While planning to compose and transmit your message in the form of a circular or notice, one must keep in mind the primary purpose is to inform your intended readers that you control the content. So, the onus of the effectiveness of the communication rests solely on you.

As Bovée et al. (2006) point out,

'All business messages have a general purpose: to inform, to persuade, or to collaborate with your audience. This overall general purpose de terminus both the amount of audience participation you need and the amount of control you have over your message... (in order) to inform your audience, you need little interaction. Audience members absorb the information and accept or reject it, but they don't contribute to message content; you control the message.... Business messages also have a specific purpose... to help you define the specific purpose of your message, ask yourself what you hope to accomplish with your message and what your audience should do or think after receiving your message.'

While the circular and notice share the same communication purpose, a possible distinction between the two is that **a circular may be physically distributed to all the concerned employees of a company, while a notice may be posted on the notice board or company website for viewing.** In this case, the descriptive label of the message would be one or the other. Whichever form you choose to transmit your message, keep the following factors in mind to determine which one would be the most effective in terms of reception and response:

- Urgency
- Formality
- Audience expectation
- Complexity
- Confidentiality
- Emotional content
- Cost
- Your need for a permanent record

2.3.2 When and How are Circulars and Notices Written?

Circulars and notices are written in response to a need to inform the employees about changes in policy and procedure or about a new direction being taken by the company. The first thing to keep in mind, therefore, is to ensure that the information needs of your intended audience are met and, in order to do this effectively, your message must be very carefully planned, composed, and completed. *Davis and Newstrom, 2002.*

2.3.2.1 While writing circulars and notices

Analyse your purpose and audience

- What is the purpose of your message- information, persuasion, or collaboration?
- What is the specific response you want from your audience?
- Is your purpose worthwhile and realistic?
- Is this the right time to transmit this message?
- What is the composition of your primary audience- size, level of understanding, expectations, and probable reaction?

Satisfy your audience's information needs

- What does your audience need to know?
- What does your audience want to know?
- Have you provided all the necessary information and made sure that it is accurate, pertinent, and ethical?

Adapt your message to suit your audience and your purpose

- Select the most effective channel and medium.
- Consider factors like urgency, formality, complexity, confidentiality, emotional content, cost, audience expectation and your need for a permanent record.

- Adopt the audience-centred approach and emphasize the positive aspects of your message-demonstrate the benefits to responding positively to your message.
- Use a polite tone and show sensitivity by using bias-free language.

Bharat Enterprises
10, Circular Road
Delhi-123456
India
Phone: 011-987654321 Email: bharatenterprises@energy.com

Circular No.- 0112/c/12/2023
30 June 2023

Subject

Text of the Message
....
....
....

Radha Singh
Senior Manager (Mrt.)

Format/ Sample- Circular 2.1

Bharat Enterprises

10, Circular Road

Delhi-123456

Phone: 011-987654321 Email: bharatenterprises@energy.com

Notice- 0112/12/2023

Subject

Text of the Message

....

....

....

Radha Singh

Senior Manager (Mrt.)

30 June 2023

Format/ Sample- Notice 2.2

2.3.2.2 Composing Circulars and Notices

- Understand the importance of good organization of your message for your company and your audience.
- Define the main idea of the message by making a specific mention about the topic.
- Limit the scope of the message by adjusting the space and detail you allocate to major points, which usually varies according to the topic.
- Group the points by constructing an outline to visualize the relation between the ideas and the supporting material.
- Choose either a direct or an indirect approach depending on what you think the reaction of the audience will be to the message- positive, negative, or neutral.

2.3.2.3 Completing Circulars and Notices

- Evaluate content, organization, style, and tone.
- Review for readability.
- Edit for clarity and conciseness. (*Bovée et al, 2006*)

Now that we know the theory of the 'why' 'how' and 'when', let us try our hand at composing a circular and a notice. At first, familiarize ourselves with the formats that can be divided into six parts:

- The letterhead of the company
- The descriptive label of the message
- The date
- The subject line of the message
- The text of the message, and
- The details of the sender of the message

2.4 Memos and Office Orders

What are Memos and Office Orders?

Memos and office orders are forms of written, internal correspondence that flow in the downward direction and follow the formal channels of hierarchical communication in an organization. While memos are primarily addressed to concerned individual receivers, office orders, are about the individual who is the intended receiver of the action being taken. Copies may also be sent to other individuals in the organization for purposes of reference and necessary action. These are not written about routine matters but are specific responses to a particular situation that demands action. At the same time, both are non-interactive insofar as they do not usually lead to a written response from the receiver. They are, however, planned so that the outcome is a change in policy, procedure, or behaviour. *Markel, 2004.*

2.4.1 A Memo- Definition, Purpose, and Format

A memo is short for 'memorandum' that comes from the Latin word *memorare* which means to mention or tell. Therefore,

'A memo is a short, official, written statement prepared for a specific person or a committee within the organization, in order to give information about a particular matter.' (*Sinha, 2001*)

Being written, a memo is a permanent record and reference about whatever is communicated.

2.4.2 Why are Memos Written?

A memo is written to fulfil the following needs in the daily working of an organization:

- To provide information
- To issue instructions
- To convey a policy decision
- To offer suggestions
- To record or report an agreement
- To seek an explanation
- To request action, information, or suggestions

2.4.3 How are Memos Written?

Most organizations use printed memo sheets, the format of which can be into 10 parts, arranged as follows:

- The company letterhead
- The descriptive label for the communication- in this case 'memorandum
- The reference number of the memo
- The addressee(s)
- Date
- The addressor
- The subject line
- The text of the message, normally divided into points, beginning with the most important and progressing accordingly
- The signature of the addressor
- The names and designations of those to whom copies of the memo is being sent

Here are some tips to help you organize the information in the memo:

- Tell the readers exactly what they need to know
- Explain the reasons for suggesting a particular course of action
- Tell the receiver clearly, what needs to be done and when
- Organize the information in one of the following ways

1. **Chronologically**- first A happened, then B, then C. Therefore, D needs to be done.

2. **Big picture to smaller picture**- The Company is committed to equal opportunities for its employees, so Equal Opportunity Cell is being created.
3. **Cause and effect**- 'The decision of the Board of Directors to adopt and implement the equal opportunity policy for its employees, which encourages them to participate and progress, without fear has led to the creation of equal opportunity cell.
4. **Act I, Act II, Act III**- Just as with a play- the problem is stated, analysed and a solution suggested. (*Dobinan, 1998*)

Bharat Enterprises
10, Circular Road
Delhi-123456
India
Phone: 011-987654321 Email: bharatenterprises@energy.com

Memorandum

No. Date

To

From

Subject: ……………………………………………………..

Text of the Message

……………………………………………………………………………………………………

……………………………………………………………………………………………………

……………………………………………………………………………………………………

Signature

CC to

a)

b)

c)

Format/Sample- Memo 2.3

2.5 What is an Office Order?

An office order is written, formal, downward, and non-interactive communication. It is normally written when the correspondence relates to the service conditions of an employee. It relates to the employees' rights. *Markel, 2004.*

2.5.1 Why are Office Orders Written?

Office orders are normally written when one or more of the following needs to be communicated to the concerned employee.

- Withdrawing rights
- Imposing restrictions
- Making postings and transfers
- Promotions
- Retrenchment
- Granting annual increment
- Withholding annual increment
- Disciplinary action. *Markel, 2004.*

Notice how some office orders may be 'bad news' messages for the receiver. One needs to be especially careful while drafting such messages so that one does not offend the receiver. The purpose of the message is behaviour modification, and the ultimate goal is a harmonious and productive working environment. In such a message, make sure you lead up to the action you propose to take, by first clarifying the situation and also demonstrating how you are left with no other option but to take this particular action.

Bharat Enterprises
10, Circular Road
Delhi-123456
India

Phone: 011-987654321 Email: bharatenterprises@energy.com

No. Date

<u>Office Order</u>

Text of the Message

....

....

....

Signature

CC to

a)

b)

c)

Format/Sample- Office Order 2.4

2.5.2 How are Office Orders Written?

While drafting an office order, in addition to using the format given below, choose your tone and language very carefully. Some of the things to keep in mind are:

- Be courteous
- Use clear and concise language
- Give facts and reasons
- Be objective- no personal comments and biases.

The office order, unlike the memo is not addressed to the concerned receiver but it is about her/him. So, the third person is used, and details are given about the person and the action being taken.

The office order, can be divided into seven parts:

1. The company letterhead
2. The reference number of the order
3. The date
4. The descriptive label for the communication- in this case 'office order'.
5. The text of the message, which should follow sequence of information regarding the Who, What, When' and 'How'.
6. The signature of the addressor.
7. The names and designations of those to whom copies of the memo are being sent.

2.6 Notification, Agenda and Minutes

In this section, we will learn about the need, purpose and drafting of memos and office orders.

Group communication in an organization is conducted in a planned manner and one of the ways in which this planning is done is during the preparations for a meeting. A meeting is planned by considering the following:

- **Who** should attend the meeting?
- **What** needs to be discussed?
- **When** and **where** should the meeting be held?

To ensure that all the members attending the meeting contribute their optimum to the deliberations, it is necessary that they are informed about the meeting in advance so that they can come prepared. As part of the preparations for the meeting, messages in the form of **Notification** and **Agenda** are written.

2.6.1 Notification and Agenda

As per the definition, a notification is an advance notice of a meeting to all the members of the group. The notice is sent well in advance and contains the following information:

1. The details of when the meeting is scheduled, at what time, where it is to be held and how long it is expected to continue.
2. The agenda for the meeting-a detailed outline of the issues to be discussed at the meeting.

The notification and agenda are prepared by the secretary of the organization in consultation with the chairperson. Since a meeting of this kind is a part of the formal channel of communication in an organization, there is a procedure for the conduct of such a discussion. *Markel, 2004.*

2.6.2 How are Meetings Conducted?

A meeting is presided over by the chairperson who is assisted by the secretary.

2.6.3 What is the Role of the Secretary in the Meeting?

It is secretary's responsibility to conduct the meeting by ensuring the agenda is followed and completed and also taking detailed notes about the deliberations, decisions, agreements, and dissent, etc.

2.6.4 What are Minutes?

When the meeting is over, the secretary compiles these notes in the form of Minutes.

A Minute is defined as a note to 'preserve the memory' and the minutes of a meeting are a faithfully written record of the proceedings of a meeting.

If the group which is scheduled to meet on say, 31 March has already met earlier, when the secretary sends out the notice for the meeting, he will also enclose the Minutes of the previous meeting with the notification.

2.6.5 Preparing the Notification and Agenda for a Meeting

Before we look at the meeting in progress, let us first understand how the notification and agenda are prepared. You will need to include the following nine items:

1. The letterhead of the organization
2. The date on which the notice is to be sent
3. The descriptive label 'notice'/'notification'

4. The message of the notice
5. The descriptive label agenda
6. The content of the agenda
7. The designation and name of the sender
8. Details of the receivers of this message-names and designations
9. The enclosure being sent with the notice

The secretary to the chairperson, will take detailed notes on the day of the meeting. These notes will then be compiled by the secretary in the form of minutes, which will then be sent to all the members who attended the meeting, after they have been approved and signed by the chairperson.

2.6.6 Writing the Minutes

The primary skill needed for writing the minutes of a meeting are note taking, the use of reported speech and the techniques of summarizing. It will be necessary for the secretary to convert all the discussion held during the meeting into reported speech, and also sequence the suggestions, ideas, emotions, etc., in a logical manner. The minutes, when they are finally ready, follow the sequence of the agenda. This will ensure that the members are reminded of the outcome of the discussions held regarding the different issues under consideration. *Bovee. et.al, 2006.*

When drafting the minutes, keep the following in mind:

- The minutes are written in the third person and in the past tense
- The names of the contributors to the discussions need not be mentioned in the final draft
- The minutes must include the outcome of the discussion of each matter in the agenda
- Agreements, decisions, and resolutions should be stated verbatim

There are two ways in which the content of the minutes can be arranged

2.6.6.1 Minutes of Narration

In this kind of structure, the leading points of the discussion are arranged in the following manner:

a) The title of the point on the agenda

b) The statements of the chairperson regarding the matter under discussion

c) The ideas, suggestions, agreement, and dissent of the various members

d) The final resolution.

This is the sequence that would be followed for each point on the agenda.

2.6.6.2 Minutes of Resolution

In this kind of structure, only the title of the item on the agenda and the decision or resolution agreed upon would be included.

The following is the order of the different activities before, during and after a meeting:

The need for a Notice and Agenda → Proceedings → Attendance meeting → +Reading of Minutes → Passing of the Minutes → Discussion → Action Plan →→ Resolutions→ Date of Next Meeting → Minutes→→ Notice and Agenda. (*Kulkarni, 2006*).

Format: Notification Agenda and Minutes

Bharath Enterprises
10, Circular Road
Delhi-123456
India
Phone: 011-987654321 E-mail: bharathe@energy.com
30th June 2024

Notice

The conference and the subsequent meeting of the Board of Directors with the members, representatives and stakeholders of Bharath Enterprises will be held in the Rajdhani Hotel, Delhi on 31st July 2024 at 11:00 a.m. The meeting is expected to last for three days, so all those requiring assistance with transport and accommodation should contact the undersigned so that suitable arrangements can be made.
The agenda of the meeting are:

Agenda

i. Ratification of the minutes of the meeting held on 31December 2023
ii. To decide how conferences and seminars could be a regular part of the employees' work regime
iii. To deliberate on the need for building more residential units for the employees
iv. To grant a piece of land for building a school and playground for the benefit of the employees and their families
v. To work out the modalities for points mentioned in iii) and iv)
vi. Any other Matter with the permission of the Chair
vii. Vote of thanks
viii. Date of the next meeting

CC: **Signature**
i)
ii)
Enclosure: Minutes of the meeting held on 31 December 2023

Format/Sample- Notice and Agenda 2.5

Bharath Enterprises
10, Circular Road
Delhi-123456
India
Phone: 011-987654321 E-mail: bharathe@energy.com
30th June 2024

Minutes of the meeting held in the Conference Room of the Rajdhani Hotel, Delhi on 30th 2024 at 11.00 a.m.

Members present:

i. P. Shanmugham, Managing Director, Bharath Enterprises Delhi
ii. Radha Singh, Senior Manager (Movement)
iii. Gurvinder Singh, Chief Finance Officer
iv. Rinchen Bhutia, Executive Engineer (Civil)
v. Vaishali Jain, Senior Architect
vi. Arun Kumar, Chief Advisor
vii. Dr. C. N. R. Naidu, Manager, Human Resource
viii. Kiran Kumar, Secretary

The Chairperson called the meeting to deliberate on the issues mentioned in the attached agenda. Thereafter, the minutes of the meeting held on 31 December 2023 was approved and signed,
....
....
....
....
....
....
....
....

It was decided that the next meeting be held on 30th November 2024.
The meeting ended with a vote of thanks to the Chair.

Format/Sample- Minutes 2.6

2.7 External Technical Communication

2.7.1 Need and Nature of External Communication

By now you already know how letters come in the category of communication that is interactive and formal, and how business messages are planned and completed. In addition to these points, we need to think about:

2.7.2 Why am I writing this letter?

Before we think about things like structures and formats, we need to ask ourselves this basic question, which is about the content of the letter. In order to make our letter effective, we need to ask ourselves the following questions because our answer lies in one of them.

I am writing this letter to inform;
I am writing this letter to persuade;
I am writing this letter to inform and persuade.

Look at the list below to see what answer you will give to the question 'Why am I writing this letter?'

i. Do I want to clarify an idea, a process, or a procedure?
ii. Do I want to explain how something works?
iii. Will my reader understand what I want to convey?
iv. Do I want to gain support for an idea, a product, or a service?
v. Do I want action as an outcome of my letter?
vi. Will my reader modify her/his behaviour after reading my letter- do something differently?

Depending on which one of these six, in isolation or in combination you deem fit, your answer will be one of the three options, that is, to inform, to persuade and to inform and persuade.

2.7.3 Basic Strategies for Effectiveness

In this section we will look at some useful tips regarding the writing of letters. The lessons learnt from the previous chapter will be useful here.

2.7.3.1 The AIDA Technique

This is a result-oriented technique and relates to the format of the letter as a whole and each letter of this acronym refers to what outcome each part of the body of the letter should have:

A-represents **attention** and asks you to plan the opening section of your letter carefully to attract the attention of the reader.
I- represents the **interest** that your letter should generate in the mind of your reader
D- represents **desire** and encourages the reader to participate in your point of view
A- represents **action** and is a clear indication of the kind of feedback you want, that is what you want the reader to do in response to your letter.

2.7.3.2 The 'Effective Ending' Approach

To make the ending of your letter effective and get the feedback and action you want, the following should be a part of the final paragraph of your letter:

CSAD- clear statement of action desired
EA- easy action, within reach and possibility of the addressee
DA- dated action, by when the feedback should be received
RB- reader benefit- how the action performed will benefit the addressee (*Murphy et al, 2000*)

2.7.3.3 Formats- How Technical Letters are Written

Most technical letters have the following parts:

1. **Heading-Letterhead:** This will include the name and contact details such as telephone and fax numbers and e-mail or website address of the sender of the letter.
2. **Date:** Since we correspond in a global environment, and different parts of the world follow different conventions to write the date, therefore, it is convenient to follow an alphanumeric format like '15 March 2024' for your letters.
3. **Reference Number:** This is again an alpha numeric notation and helps in the filing of the letter and is also useful for reference in future correspondence in which it can be quoted to help the receiver. This is a descriptive label and will be named in the letter.
4. **Inside Address:** This will include the name and the address of the proposed addressee of the letter. Remember to include the designation along with the name if your letter is meant for a specific individual.
5. **Subject Line:** This should be a short phrase that indicates the purpose or desired outcome of your letter.
6. **Salutation:** You can choose to use 'Dear' or simply write Madam/ Sir or the name of the addressee. Remember to use the surname as this is a formal communication.
7. **Body:** Details of the communication is to be included here.

8. **Complementary Close:** You can use 'truly' or 'sincerely', use 'yours' only if you used 'dear' in the salutation.

9. **Signature Area:** Remember to sign, write your name in block letters below your signature and mention your designation

10. **Enclosure Notation:** This is a descriptive label and will be named in the letter.

Keep the following guidelines in mind when composing a business letter.

Let us look now at the different ways in which the letter can be formatted.

1. The quality of the paper used.
2. The colour of the paper and the ink-black on white or cream is the best.
3. Careful labelling of the envelope with all the information complete and in acceptable manner with your address on the top or bottom left hand, complete address of the addressee in the centre.

2.8 Financial Communication

Pre-reading Activity

The same provisional store that you had inherited from your father (the details can be found in pre-reading activity of the section 2.1.3), has now become a growing organization called Bharath Enterprises with an annual turnover of Rs 100 crore. It has customers across the length and breadth of the world and corresponds regularly with banks and insurance agencies for its financial needs and claims, and also undertakes import-export related correspondence.

While there are customers who make payments regularly, there are also defaulters who fail to make their payments on time. Radha Singh as the senior sales manager is constantly confronted with complaints from sales manager and the Retail sales manager. Let us now look at how Radha Singh deals with customers who default on their payments.

2.8.1 Collection Letters

The collection department of Bharath Enterprises will correspond with defaulting customers. It is important to retain goodwill, so the letters will be courteous and cordial. For these letters, we will use a combination of the direct and indirect approaches.

The letters are normally written in three stages, progressively, depending on the response received: Mild Reminders → Persuasive Letters- Last Resort Letters.

2.8.1.1 Stage 1: Mild Reminders

This is also known as the will pay stage, as the company is confident of receiving the payment. This letter is a reminder to the customer and will be a 'direct approach' letter and will include the following points:

i. Details of the transaction: date, size of consignment, a copy of the invoice/statement of account.

ii. This is the first reminder, so the words 'please' and just a friendly reminder can be used.

iii. The letter closes with easy, dated action, asking for the payment.

iv. The concluding statement reiterates the appreciation for the business and the anticipation of continued interaction.

Two or three such mild reminders may be sent, depending on company policy and the past record of the customer. Each successive letter will, in addition to the above points, make a reference to the letters already sent. *Business English, 2007.*

2.8.1.2 Stage 2: Persuasive Letters

This is the 'should pay stage' and is needed if no reply has been received to the mild reminders sent. At this stage, we need to persuade the customer to make the payment and will need to appeal to her/his conscience, concern for reputation etc. Since this is a persuasive letter, it will use the indirect approach, and we can offer an incentive or concession to motivate positive action. *Business English, 2007.*

When we reach this stage, we have not received any reply to our mild reminders and will need to be as persuasive as possible. We include the following points in the following sequence, to make it more effective:

- The buffer: an attention getting opening- an attractive incentive offer.
- An appeal to the receiver's conscience, social prestige, reputation in the market, etc.
- A suggestion to help the customer solve any problem that is causing non-payment.
- A mention of the mild reminders sent earlier.
- A clear request for payment.
- A courteous close with easy-dated action.

Again, depending on company policy and the importance of the customer to the affected organization, two or three such persuasive letters may be sent.

2.8.1.3 Stage 3: Last Resort Letters

This is the final stage in the correspondence relating to collection of outstanding payments and is known as the 'must pay stage'.

We reach this stage when all reminders, appeals and suggestions have failed and we have no resort but to write a 'direct approach' letter, giving the defaulting customer one last chance to pay. This letter will be short and to the point and will include the following points

1. Details of the transaction and the amount outstanding.
2. Mention of the reminders and offers made.
3. A final chance to make the payment immediately.
4. The future course of action if the payment is not made.
5. A courteous close with easy action.

As in the case of the reminders and persuasive letters, every organization has its own policy regarding collection of outstanding payments.

2.8.2 Communication with Banks

As Bharath Enterprises expands its operations, it needs financial support and for this it relies heavily on banks. In addition to generating funds, the company will need to regularly correspond with its bank for various commercial transactions.

Some of the situations that demand correspondence are

- Opening a current account
- Stopping payment for a cheque
- Request for an overdraft
- Request for a loan
- Request for a bank guarantee
- Request for a current accounts statement
- Request for the opening of a letter of credit.

These are normally direct approach letter and depending on the credit worthiness of an organization, a 'good news' response can be expected. Most of these are fairly routine requests that the bank will have no hesitation in agreeing to. In some cases, however, the bank may send a 'bad news' letter, in which case the company has to make the necessary effort to persuade the bank to comply with its request. For this, the company will need to prepare the necessary proof of its credit worthiness to receive a 'good news' response. In such a situation, the letters will follow the persuasive 'indirect approach', in hope of positive feedback. *Business English, 2007.*

2.8.3 Communication with Insurance Agencies

By definition, Insurance is an agreement that in return for small, regular payments made, the agency will compensate the company for loss, damage, injury, or death (*Sinha, 2001*) The four main kinds of insurance are:

- Fire insurance
- Accident insurance
- Marine insurance
- Life insurance.

Every organization takes out an insurance policy for its Business transactions, its premises, and its employees. This removes the element of uncertainty from business and allows the organization to take some commercial risks with the confidence of a 'cover'. Insurance is also an incentive for employees who dedicate their lives and efforts to build the company. Insurance correspondence normally relates to three kinds of needs:

- Asking for a policy to be prepared for a specific need.
- Asking for an assessment to be made for the loss suffered.
- Asking for settlement of a claim or compensation.

While most of these are routine letters and follow the direct approach, sometimes persuasive letters need to be written, using the indirect approach. The most important element of insurance correspondence is clarity about facts and figures. These facts and figures will make your letter complete and ensure that you get positive feedback from receiver of your letter.

2.9 Employment Related Communication

Let us familiarize ourselves with the job application process and learn how to respond to a job advertisement, write a resume/biodata/curriculum vitae.

2.9.1 A Personal Swot Analysis

The first step in the job application process is for you to analyse yourself carefully in terms of the following:

- Skills
- Accomplishments
- Interests
- Personal values

This self-analysis will help you to decide what kind of work you would like to do and also to communicate your suitability for a particular job in a competitive employment environment. Let us look each one of them.

1. **Skills**

These indicate the areas of your professional and academic expertise and will help you to match your qualifications with the requirements of the job. Here is a list of useful verbs that you can use to enumerate your skills. These are illustrative and you can replace them with another appropriate verb. The important thing to remember is to begin with the verb and follow it with a statement elaborating on the action implied.

Examples:

Analysing Administering Consulting Planning Evaluating Coordinating Negotiating Mediating Creating Speaking

Activity
The best way is to write a sentence about your skills, beginning each with one of the verbs given above.

For example: While I was secretary of the College Literary Association, I **negotiated** with the management for an additional literature section in the library.

2. **Accomplishments**

Even as a fresh graduate, you would have a host of personal and academic, even professional accomplishments that you can write about, in support of your application. The important thing to do is **to state not only your accomplishment, but also its outcome.**

For example: Joining the National Service Scheme in college helped me to become sensitive to the needs of those less fortunate than me.

Notice in the above sentence, you have not only talked about an accomplishment, which is joining the NSS, but also talked about how this contributed to the development of your character.

Here is an illustrative list of verbs to help you write about your accomplishments:

Winning Joining Increasing Obtaining Travelling Reading Studying Started Completing Learning

> **Activity**
> *Using this list of verbs, write 10 sentences about your accomplishments. Here analyse your confidence and satisfaction in relation to each of your accomplishments The areas of insecurity and dissatisfaction are those that you need to work on.*

3. Interests

Analysing your interests, attitudes and aptitude will help you to decide for which type of job you can best use your skills. Here are some questions you can ask yourself:

- Which jobs have I most enjoyed doing and why?
- Do I prefer to work with figures, machines, people, or ideas?
- Which things have brought me the most satisfaction?
- Which hobbies have I enjoyed the most?

4. Personal Values

Every good organization has the commitment to create an ethical environment. You will have your own ethical parameters and entering the job market is a good time to think once again about your personal values. Remember that every organization is as good as its employees, and you can make a significant contribution by enriching the organization with your values. Some of the important personal values are:
Altruism-Prestige-Adventure-Harmony-Power-Independence-Money-Physical Activity-Egalitarianism (*Murphy et al., 2000*)

> ***Activity:*** *Make a profile of your personal value system using some or all of the words You could also arrange them in descending order of priority, beginning with t consider most important.*

2.9.2 Writing your Resume/Biodata/Curriculum Vitae

Resume or biodata is a necessary annexure to any job application. It is a document that lists the personal details, objectives, and achievements of a person in a simple format. There is, as such, no standard format for a resume. The most important thing to remember while drafting a resume is the purpose- the task that you expect the resume to accomplish. Therefore, apart from being informative, the resume must also be persuasive. This is not an overt persuasiveness, rather the arrangement of data in a manner that makes the document focused and convincing. You could consider the following points to make the resume effective.

- Use headings for the separate sections of the resume.
- Use phrases in point form rather than full sentences.
- Refer to those aspects first which have a direct relationship with the application that you are preparing.
- Be positive in the choice of terms, not hesitant.
- Arrange those items first where you have more achievements. The resume could be thematically arranged under different headings or be chronological, that is, the entries could be organized according to dates. In the latter aspect, the preference may be given to reverse chronology, that is, the latest entry is listed first.

Business English, 2007.

2.9.3 Consider these headings for a basic resume for job applications

- Personal data
- Contact information
- Statement of professional objectives
- Work experience
- Academic and professional qualification
- Extra-curricular activities
- References

1. Personal Data

Under this heading include:

- Name
- Date of Birth

2. Contact Information

The thumb-rule here is to include all the contact data that can help reach you fastest. The easier it is to respond, the greater the chances of the contacting you.

- Contact address
- Telephone: landline, mobile
- E-mail

3. Statement of Professional Objectives

Mention your career objective in a short statement on the basis of your own self-analysis as well as the job you are applying for.

4. Work Experience

List your work experience starting with your current job first, mentioning the name of organization, position held, nature of post, work responsibilities and period of work.

5. Academic and Professional Qualifications

Arrange your academic qualifications and professional qualifications separately again with the most recent ones coming first. You should mention the name of course, the examination passed, and year of passing, institution and results. A special distinction achieved may also be pointed out. You could use a tabular format, too.

6. Extra-curricular activities

Under this heading list all those activities and achievements which help projecting you as a person with a range of interests. Remember to include awards from school and college, positions held, social service initiatives taken and publications.

7. References

Do not give too many references. Two or three should suffice. You should seek prior consent of your referees before you actually give their names. Provide their postal addresses, e-mail, telephone numbers, etc., so that they are easily contactable. Try and provide a variety of referees from your teachers, supervisors in the workplace or business friends.

RESUME

Personal Data

Name

Date of Birth

Contact Information

Address

Telephone

Fax

E-mail
Objective
Work Experience
Educational Qualification
Extra-curricular Activities
References
Signature
Date

Format/Sample- Resume 2.7

2.9.4 Writing the Job Application Letter

You have already learned how to write your resume. Along with the resume you will need to send a cover letter. Its purpose is to attract the interest of your prospective employer, to call you for an interview. While writing this letter, we will follow the format we have already learned. We will keep the tone reader-centric and also include evidence to support all the claims we are making.

2.9.4.1 The Opening-Favourable Attention

The contemporary communication theories support these three as being most effective for beginning a job application letter:

- **A Summary Opening** Give a two-three sentence summary of your most outstanding qualifications related to the job you are seeking.

  For example: Bharat Enterprises and Hindustan Electricals- both these organizations gave me the opportunity to apply my technical skills earned in college. For two years I was also given the responsibility of being the treasurer of the college union and this gave me the opportunity to hone my communication skills.

- **A Source Opening** A reference to how you learned about this job opportunity. For example: Your advertisement in the Times Classified Section of 11 March 2024, suggested the need for a technical consultant. My academic training in engineering and work experience in the field of mechanical and electrical workshop makes me a suitable candidate for the job.

- **A Question Opening** You can begin with a question that demonstrates your understanding of the company's need and your ability to fulfil that need.

  For example: Is Bharat Enterprises in need of a good Assistant Engineer? I am an engineering graduate with very good communication skills. I have also worked in the the field of mechanical and electrical workshop, and this make me a suitable candidate to fulfil the need.

2.9.4.2 Middle Paragraph- Data and Details

The middle paragraph of your letter will be divided into three sections

- Education
- Work Experience
- Personal Details - attitudes, interests, activities, qualities

Let us now look at each of these in turn to see how we can communicate this personal data in the most effective manner possible.

1. **Education**
   - How did your overall education prepare you for the work you seek? Demonstrate a broad-based understanding of the discipline (Engineering) along with an in-depth knowledge of certain areas (AUTO-CAD and JAVA).
   - Give details of any extra educational qualifications you have in addition to the course you graduated in. Did you do any courses that complement your knowledge in the areas of accounts and communication?

2. **Work Experience**
   - State how you gained practical experience in addition to your education.
   - How did you adapt to different working environments?
   - Did you accomplish anything special in any of the tasks assigned to you?

3. **Personal Details**
   - How well do you work in a group, towards the fulfilment of a shared goal?
   - How can you prove your sustained interest in your chosen field?
   - Can you demonstrate any special commitment or quality that shows determination, initiative, integrity, etc.?

2.9.4.3 Closing Paragraph

Easy action makes it clear that you are asking for a call for an interview. Give details of how and when you can be reached-by phone, e-mail, etc.

2.9.5 Checklist: An Effective Job Application Letter

Here are a few essential themes and layout tips that can help you in creating a good cover letter.

- Read the advertisement carefully and understand what the company is looking for in the prospective job candidate.
- The cover letter should be concise and to the point (usually one page).
- It should be addressed formally and to the most appropriate person in the organization.
- The letter should be formatted well with proper spacing.
- Leave about six or seven lines blank at the top of the page.
- If you know who should be contacted, mention the person's name beginning with 'Dear'. If not, address and begin your letter with 'Dear Sir or Madam' and end with "Yours faithfully.
- Pay attention to the heading of the cover letter, as it informs the reader which job you are applying for. Use bold for this line.
- In the first paragraph, you should introduce yourself and say why you are writing to them and why you want to work for them. Further, you should include the most promising points from your CV which will help you to market yourself.
- Mention some of your most relevant job experiences which can show that you have experience in the field and skills to match the requirements.

The cover letter is supposed to create an interest in the reader to study your CV. So do not go overboard and mention everything again in your cover letter. Show the employer that you are interested in being interviewed for the advertised position by mentioning something like- 'I look forward to hearing from you'. Add your contact details on the cover letter so that the employer can contact you easily without having to hunt for your details. Include your address, phone no, email ID etc., Since you are attaching your resume with the letter, it is a good practice to mention Enclosure: 'Curriculum Vitae' on the last line of your cover letter. Now, sign and write the date in your letter.

Unit Summary

In this chapter you have learnt:

Correspondence is important for the functioning, growth, and success of an organization.

- *Today's global work environment has made communication challenging due to several reasons: technical, economic, and psychological.*
- *Communication is always a two-way process: internal correspondence is non-interactive in nature and flows in the downward direction from management to employee(s): external correspondence is interactive in nature and sets up a series of interactions between the organization and the potential existing consumers of its goods and services.*
- *A notification is advance information about a meeting sent to all the members. It contains details of when and where the meeting is to be held and also how long it is expected to continue.*
- *The notification of the meeting also includes an agenda that gives a list of all the matters to be discussed at the meeting.*
- *The meeting is presided over by a chairperson who is assisted by a secretary.*
- *The secretary prepares the notification and agenda, in consultation with the chairperson and sends it to the members in advance of the meeting.*
- *During the meeting, the secretary takes detailed notes and compiles these in the form of minutes.*
- *Minutes are the official record of the proceedings of the meeting, as well as the resolutions adopted and the action plan decided upon.*
- *The first thing to do in the job application process is self-analysis and list your strengths and weaknesses with regard to your skills, accomplishments, interests, and values.*

- *An effective resume gives a summary of your qualifications and your work experience and also provides the necessary personal details about you.*
- *The job application letter accompanies the resume.*
- *The opening paragraph of this letter should get favourable attention. You can*
- *use one of three openings-summary, source or question.*
- *The middle paragraph of your letter contains data and details to education, work experience and your personal details like attitudes, interests, activities and qualities. The closing paragraph asks for easy action-the call for an interview.*

Exercises:

Multiple Choice:

1. Which of the following is NOT a function of effective communication in an organization?
   a. Clear and condense information
   b. Highlight and focus on key issues
   c. Increase ambiguity in messages
   d. Persuade to change behaviour or notions

2. Which of the following is a common form of non-interactive correspondence?
   a. Emails between coworkers
   b. Circulars to employees
   c. Customer feedback forms
   d. Social media posts

3. Select the correct statement:
   a. Non-interactive correspondence includes memos and office orders.
   b. Interactive correspondence is typically internal to an organization.
   c. Non-interactive correspondence is always external.
   d. Interactive correspondence does not expect any response.

4. Which of the following is NOT a component of an organizational chart?
   a. Chain of command
   b. Employee responsibilities
   c. Marketing strategies
   d. Company aspirations

5. What is a key principle of effective internal organizational communication?
    a. Limiting communication to only essential updates
    b. Ensuring only managers have access to the strategic plan
    c. Developing sound meeting management skills
    d. Avoiding feedback from employees to prevent confusion

6. Select the correct statement:
    a. Downward communication is only used to delegate tasks to employees.
    b. Circulars are addressed to individual employees.
    c. Upward communication includes regular status reports from employees to their supervisors.

7. The AIDA technique in letter writing stands for:
    a. Attention, Interest, Desire, Action
    b. Attention, Information, Detail, Action
    c. Acknowledge, Interest, Decision, Action
    d. Attention, Interest, Decision, Action

8. Which of the following is NOT a part of the business letter format?
    a. Salutation
    b. Body
    c. Greeting
    d. Enclosure notation

9. Select the correct statement:
    a. The purpose of a resume is to explain your hobbies in detail.
    b. The cover letter should repeat all the information in the resume.
    c. A cover letter should be concise and to the point.
    d. Resumes should only list educational qualifications, not work experience.

10. Identify the correct statement about the modified block format
    a. All parts of the letter are aligned to the left margin.
    b. The date and closing are aligned to the right margin.
    c. There are no paragraphs in this format.
    d. It uses a decorative font.

Answers: 1-c, 2-b, 3-a, 4-c, 5-c, 6-c, 7-a, 8-c, 9-c, 10-b

Subjective Questions

1. Define 'interactive correspondence' in a business context.
2. List any three challenges faced by organisation in terms of communication in the contemporary times.
3. Why is written communication considered valuable and technical activities?
4. Explain the importance of having an effective communication network within an organization.
5. Write an essay on the role of technical correspondence in building organizational credibility and stakeholders' trust.
6. Discuss how advances in technology have impacted the speed, frequency, and reach of technical communication.
7. Define a business organizational chart. Draw a flow chart to explain it.
8. Differentiate between a circular and a notice.
9. List three essential elements to include when drafting minutes of a meeting.
10. Write an essay on the importance of effective internal communication within an organization.

Know More

- *Daniel McCallum developed an organisational chart for the New York and Erie Railroad in 1854. This diagram improves communication and boosts output by detailing the roles and duties of every person in the organisation.*

- *Memos have been a crucial component of business communication since the start of the 20th century. Memos were the primary method of internal communication during World War II since they were necessary for optimal organisational results.*

- *Research indicates that the manner and comprehensibility of internal communication may substantially influence employees' psychological well-being. Positive, unambiguous, and succinct communication correlates with heightened productivity and work contentment.*

- *The emergence of e-mail brought about a significant transformation in commercial communication. Nevertheless, even with the increasing prevalence of digital communication, conventional mediums such as memoranda and letters continue to possess substantial importance, particularly in official and legal settings.*

- *Cultural sensitivity in correspondence is of utmost importance in the modern globalised era, as it is essential to comprehend and respect cultural disparities in communication. For instance, direct communication is highly regarded in the United States, but in several Asian cultures, indirect communication is often favoured. This preference significantly influences how business communications are formulated.*

- *The decision to use interactive or non-interactive communication is often based on the kind of information being delivered. Interactive communication is well-suited for receiving feedback and engaging in discussions, while non-interactive communication efficiently provides explicit and unequivocal instructions.*

- *The legal significance of business communication lies in its potential to serve as crucial evidence in legal disputes, leading many firms to preserve such documents. Prudent composition of letters and e-mails may avoid misinterpretations and safeguard the company's legal concerns.*

- *The structure and style of financial letters have substantially evolved over the years. Currently, digital technologies enable the creation of more interactive displays of financial data; nevertheless, the fundamental standards of clarity and accuracy remain unaltered.*

- *A well-designed job application or résumé may substantially influence hiring choices. Studies suggest recruiters often develop perceptions within the first 6 seconds of seeing a curriculum vitae, highlighting the need for succinct and influential information.*

- *Artificial Intelligence is progressively used to compose and evaluate commercial communication. Artificial intelligence (AI) techniques may assist in guaranteeing that communication is unambiguous, free from mistakes, and culturally suitable; however, human supervision is still crucial for preserving the personal aspect.*

References and Suggested Readings

Weiss, E. H. (2015). The elements of international English style: A guide to writing correspondence, reports, technical documents, and internet pages for a global audience. Routledge.

Sharma, R. C., & Mohan, K. (2016). Business Correspondence and Report Writing: A Practical Approach to Business & Technical Communication.

Dynamic QR Coding for Further Readings

Business Correspondence

SWOT Analysis

Biodata/ Curriculum Vitae (CV)

Cover Letter

3 E- Communication

Unit Specifics

In today's world, it is essential to learn how to interact in a way that reflects our positive attitudes. That is why manners, etiquette and other social skills form an important part of our upbringing. Effective communication, whether it is verbal, nonverbal or written, is an art that requires learning and assimilation. With changing times and advances in technology, methods of communication have changed in more ways than one. Pick up a telephone and you are connected to your friends or relatives immediately. Write an e-mail and the message is transmitted within a few seconds. One of the common methods of communication that is very popular and quick is the electronic medium. In the earlier unit you learnt about written technical communication. In this unit we shall deal with the electronic medium of communication prevalent in the contemporary world. Along with e-writing, other modes of communication like groupware, telecom technology, e-commerce, etc., will be discussed in this unit.

Apart from this at the end of the unit, a succinct recapitulation of the overall broad concepts is provided in the form of a unit summary. Besides, a large number of multiple-choice questions as well as descriptive type questions are included. A list of suggested readings are given in the unit so that one can go through them for practice. It is important to note that for getting more information on various topics of interest some QR codes have been provided which can be scanned for relevant and additional knowledge.

Rationale

In the contemporary world, E- correspondence has become a vital part of our communication process. As you know this process is operated by the Internet. Therefore, it is imperative to understand the principles governing this process.

Pre-requisites

Before reading this unit, the students are advised to revisit the following:

Employability Skills Class XII, Chapter 1 Communication Skills, NCERT

Fundamental Idea of E- correspondence, Internet, teleconferencing, online platforms for various study and business purposes

Basic reading of Unit I and II of this book

Unit Outcomes

After studying this unit, students will be able to:

U3-O1: *Manage different types of meetings effectively, which includes understanding the roles of the chairperson and participants.*

U3-O2: *Plan and conduct productive group discussions, setting clear objectives and managing diverse opinions.*

U3-O3: *Prepare and deliver engaging oral presentations with structured content and effective visual aids.*

U3-O4: *Handle question-and-answer sessions confidently, responding clearly and managing challenging questions.*

U3-O5: *Apply effective communication strategies, adapting content to the audience and using nonverbal cues.*

U3-O6: *Use digital tools and technologies to enhance presentations and communication activities professionally.*

Unit-3 Outcomes	**EXPECTED MAPPING WITH COURSE OUTCOMES** *(1- Weak Correlation; 2- Medium correlation; 3- Strong Correlation)*					
	CO-1	**CO-2**	**CO-3**	**CO-4**	**CO-5**	**CO-6**
U3-O1	2	1	2	3	2	2
U3-O2	2	1	2	3	2	2
U3-O3	3	2	3	2	3	3
U3-O4	3	1	3	3	3	2
U3-O5	3	2	3	3	3	2
U3-O6	2	2	2	2	2	3

Principles of Communication and E-Correspondence

Pre-reading Activity

Think it over:

- All living creatures communicate in some way or the other. How do animals communicate.
- How is animal communication different from human communication?
- How does language make us different from other creatures?
- Why do we need to communicate?
- Can you think of two kinds of technologies that enable us to communicate?

3.1 Communication and Language

In today's world it is important to communicate quickly, clearly, and efficiently as organizations have to build products, run operations, and deliver services in a way which is better, faster and cheaper. Modern technological tools enable us to perform in an efficient manner. Their level of efficiency and effectiveness depends upon how we use them. Not only do they help both individuals and groups to deal with routine writing tasks, but these aids also enhance and assist our creative thinking process. We use language for various purposes, which include communicating information, ideas, and emotions.

3.2. Communicating information

To influence other people through the use of words which can either persuade directly or indirectly without the receiver being conscious of it- advertisers and politicians often use language in the way that it acts as a tool:

- To regulate our actions. For instance, teachers and doctors often tell us what to do.
- To entertain through the humorous, poetic use of language.

- To record something in a way that helps us to organize our work. It could be a shopping list, a ledger, or an attendance register, or even a diary.

3.3 Principles of Communication

There are certain principles of communication to be applied while composing effective technical messages. These principles furnish guidelines for choosing the content and style of presentation, which are suited to the purpose and receiver of the message. The **7 Cs of communication** (*Murphy et al, 2000*), which form the backbone of any kind of writing, are given below.

3.3.1 Clarity

Be clear about what you want to convey to your intended recipient. Then, select your words carefully in order to make sense and sound appropriate to the reader. Do not use complex or high-sounding and pretentious words which may be unfamiliar to the reader. Your sentences should be of 17-20 words in length. Use paragraphs to state your views clearly so that no one has to read it twice to understand it. Each paragraph should convey one thought and also be linked to me next paragraph by means of a common thread of thought.

Use the appropriate level of formality. Technical communication usually requires a moderate or highly formal style. Begin all correspondence with a suitable salutation and end similarly. Be tactful, thoughtful, and respectful. Use non-discriminatory expressions that reflect equal treatment of people regardless of gender, colour, ethnic origin and physical features. Be especially careful when communicating with people of other cultures.

3.3.2 Conciseness

This quality is a prerequisite for technical communication. It is important to use fewer and effective words rather than be verbose and wordy. Conciseness saves time and money of both reader and sender. Therefore, include only relevant material and avoid any unnecessary repetition.

Examples of Wordy sentences and phrases

1. In due course.
2. Please find attached the file you requested.
3. It was realized by Mr. Kumar that we must reduce inventory.
4. There are four rules that must be observed.
5. The issue of most relevance is teamwork.

Examples of corresponding concise sentences/phrases

1. Soon
2. The file you requested is attached.
3. Mr Kumar realized; we must reduce the inventory.
4. Four rules must be observed.
5. The most relevant issue is team.

3.3.3 Concreteness

This means being specific, definite and vivid rather than vague and general. The receiver of the communication should know what is required, desired, or intended. Use active verbs more than passive ones in your writing. However, in some cases it may be more appropriate to use the passive voice, especially when it may be rude or unwise to specify a particular person (instead of writing you failed to include, you could say 'the final report was not included with the other papers').

3.3.4 Consideration

It means writing all messages with due consideration to the reader. You should keep in mind the problems, circumstances, emotions, and probable reactions of the reader to your request. This is called the 'you attitude' wherein the focus is on the reader that is, 'you', instead of 'I' and 'we'.

'We' oriented statement: I am happy to announce that we will be extending our services by an hour to make shopping more convenient.

'You' oriented statement: 'You will be able to shop in the evenings with the extended hours'.

3.3.5 Completeness

A technical message is complete when it has all the facts and data the read requires for the reaction you want or desire. This offers the benefit of generating goodwill, averts expensive lawsuits that may result if complete information missing. Answer all questions that have been asked and provide all necessary information the reader needs for correct understanding.

3.3.6 Correctness

This requires using proper grammar, spelling and punctuation in technical communications. It also means using accurate facts, figures, and words, as well as using the right level of language.

3.3.7 Comprehensiveness

This means that you should write in a way that discusses all ideas you wish to communicate, answers all queries and doubts (if raised), and the reader is able to grasp the main points of the message/document.

Features of Technical E-correspondence

The following qualities should be a part of any technical e-correspondence:

1. *The language should be simple, vivid and appealing in nature.*
2. *A dull, stilted and stiff tone is likely to put off the receiver. Instead, use a friendly conversational tone.*
3. *Be clear in your thought and expression.*
4. *Project a 'you' attitude. Write all communication keeping the reader in mind. Show interest in her/him.*
5. *Use polite expressions and a courteous style.*
6. *Adopt a persuasive tone.*
7. *Do not use jargon, clichés and slang.*

8. *Use active voice as far as possible.*
9. *Your business communication should reflect your sincerity and honesty.*
10. *Your choice of words should reveal a positive attitude.*
11. *Highlight all important facts and points.*
12. *Your writing should be coherent, meaningful and comprehensive.*
13. *Your writing should reflect your genuine feelings.*
14. *Avoid culturally insensitive words.*

Arredondo, 2003

3.4 Internet

In today's era, the importance of communication and information and hence the Internet can hardly be overemphasized. With the advent of the Internet, information has become a mass resource, that is, it is available in abundance. Now, the problem is dealing sensibly with the huge amount of information and how to make a good use of it. There is also the need to update one's skills when you are a student or looking for a job. It is important to have secure, relevant, and accurate information in your field of specialization and to share this information with others. Here the Internet comes to the rescue.

Can you imagine your life without the Internet? From paying the online bills and fees, ordering articles, online classes, securing admissions to contacting anyone that you want to, the Internet always comes to the rescue. It is a worldwide system of interconnected computer networks- 'a publicly accessible network of networks' that transmit data by using the standard Internet Protocol (IP). Through a computer, modem and an Internet Service Provider (ISP) OR Wifi, a company which provides access to the Internet, one can reach the Internet.

The World Wide Web is the most popular service on the Internet and a reference resource that is unrivalled in both the virtual and the real world. It is the most important ingredient or application that has made the Internet commercially viable. It emerged in the early 1990s and hence it is more recent than the Internet. It is the Web which provides access to billions of pages or documents through the medium of the Internet and is created in a language called **HTML-Hyper Text Mark-up Language**. These pages contain information which includes text, graphics, animation, and other objects. Then there are browsers like **Google Chrome, Mozilla Firefox** which access web documents called **web pages** that are linked to each other via **hyperlinks.** The Web is just one of the ways by which information can be disseminated over the Internet. In fact, it has added colour, voice and video to the Internet as well as created or generated an infrastructure of communications and information. The Internet is used for other services, too, like e-mail, news groups, instant messaging, online lectures and so on and so forth. Therefore, the Web is just a part of the Internet, albeit a large one, but the two terms are not synonymous and should not be confused. Search engines, like Yahoo!, Google, and keyword-based Internet research, help millions of people worldwide to have easy, instant access to a vast and diverse range of online information. The World Wide Web has created a sudden and extreme decentralization of information and data as compared with traditional libraries and encyclopaedias. *Booher, 2007.*

3.4.1 Differences Between Internet and World Wide Web- WWW

The Internet is a massive group of interconnected computer networks that are linked by copper wires, fibre-optic cables, wireless connections, etc. On other hand, the Web is a way of accessing information through the medium of the Internet. It is an information sharing model or an application layer built on top of the Internet.

The Internet consists of an infrastructure of networks linking millions of computers and mobiles all over the world. Whereas the Web is a collection of interconnected documents and other resources, linked by hyperlinks and URLs. It is one of the services available on the Internet, along with other services including e-mail, social media platforms etc. *Booher, 2007.*

Information travels over the Internet through various languages called protocols. The Web uses only one language, that is, http protocol which allows data transmission and applications to communicate to share information and exchange information.

3.4.2 Internet Protocol (IP): Domain Name System (DNS)

In its early days, one computer could connect to another by providing the IP address of the latter, which has numeric denotation. At that time computers were connected with modems and telephone lines. However, with the increase in the number of hosts or online systems it became too cumbersome to manage this task. The solution to the problem came in the form of maintaining a simple text file that mapped names to IP addresses. With the passage of time, even this text file became too large to wield. The use of the **Domain Name System DNS** (created by the University of Wisconsin 1983) made it easy to connect to other computers as this system automatically maps text names to IP addresses. Now, you need to remember the web address only, that is, www.bharathenterprises.com instead of its IP address. *Booher, 2007.*

3.4.3 Uniform Resource Locators

When you visit a website, the first screen that you see is the home page. Each page in a website has a unique address known as the Uniform Resource Locator URL. The top-level domain (TLD) name or first-level domain name is written after the period, in an abbreviated form, ie. Com (company). Some other TLDs are

info (general information)
edu (education)
gov (government)
net (network resources)
org (non-profit organizations)

3.4.4 Local Area Network (LAN)

Though the Internet has grown at a phenomenal rate, local area networks remain distinct. These are computer networks that extend to a few kilometres and are cost-effective and efficient as they do not require the setting up of all the features associated with larger networks.

3.4.4.1 Intranet

The Internet uses a set of protocols called TCP/IP (Transmission Control Protocol/ Internet Protocol). There are two adaptations of Internet technology—the intranet and the extranet- which make use of these protocols. The Intranet is a private internal company-based network which can be accessed only by members or employees of an organization, regardless of their actual location. Anyone surfing the Internet cannot get into such a company-bound site. The reasons for the popularity of intranets are more than one. The need to have more information about the company, the flexibility and convenience of use, and the desire to share global knowledge, has fuelled the movement to intranets.

By using Intranet facilities an institute's/college's/ company's records and related information can be made available on the intranet. The organization can store on it directories, customer information, employee skills lists, project status reports, company calendars and events and other records so that they are accessible from anywhere in the world using an Internet connection and a password (*Bovee et al 2006*).

We all access intranet facilities in our university/institute campuses which is available only inside/ vicinity of the campus and members of the campus community are allowed to access it. We are given an ID and a password to access this facility.

3.4.4.2 Extranet

The extranet 'is an external Intranet that allows people to communicate and exchange data within a secure network (*Bovee et al., 2006*). It permits other qualified people from outside (other than employees) such as suppliers and customers, to access this network using a password. Thus, extranets can save companies a lot of time and money because they favor quick and easy communication with clients, suppliers, or colleagues. Moreover, updated information is available on time besides being easily accessible.

3.5 Technical/Business Use of the Internet

- Gain access to global information.
- Share text, photos, video clips, slides and other data with anyone and everyone.

- Its flexibility and access permit people to work away from the office. They can work from home or while on the move. Remaining in online contact for work and education became a necessity during the covid-19 pandemic. During the same period of the pandemic, we had practical experience of how useful Internet is- be it attending online classes on google classrooms or attending meetings, it was all done with the help of the Internet.
- Conduct e-commerce activities
- Conduct electronic learning or e-learning through the use of computers and Internet. By now we all have become experts in attending online classes due to the covid 19 pandemic. It is a way of teaching and learning which lends itself naturally to distance learning and flexible learning. However, a judicious mix of e-learning and face-to-face teaching or learning (termed as blended learning) can be effectively used.

According to Naidu, 'E-learning is commonly referred to the international use of networked information and communications technology in teaching and learning. Several other terms are also used to describe this mode of teaching and learning. They include online learning, virtual learning, distributed learning, network and web-based learning." (*Naidu, 2016*).

3.5.1 Instant Messaging

It has the following features:

- **Instant messages-** Exchange of notes/information back and forth with a friend who is online.
- **Chat-**Create a chat room with friends or co-workers or through social media platforms like X (Twitter), Instagram, WhatsApp etc. these media are also suitable for sharing files and links, audio messages, videos, pictures etc.
- **Streaming content-**watch real-time news through platforms like YouTube and Facebook live etc.

3.5.2 Challenges to the Internet

- Information overload has seen organizations being flooded with documents of all kinds so much so that employees are unable to discriminate between important, useful, and useless information.
- Data security is a matter of grave concern. Attempts are always made to infiltrate company networks from outside to steal, destroy or change data. This is called hacking and those who attempt it are called hackers. When company networks are invaded for non-destructive reasons, that is, for showing off one's talent or playing a trick, it is called cracking. Another serious threat is cyber-terrorism, when company or government networks are broken into for political or economic reasons.
- Introducing viruses and predatory software.

To counter these threats, organisations have to take adequate security measures:

- Software programs can be used to screen e-mail messages from cyber threats.
- All computers should have proper password protection
- Organisations should install anti-virus software/programs to eliminate the incidence of virus attacks.
- Security software such as firewalls can be installed so that only those users who present the proper password and system identification can access the networks.
- Organisations should also screen their own employees and decide which of them should receive passwords for accessing vital company information.
- Organisations may adopt a security policy which requires employees to use passwords, switch off computers when not in use, encrypt sensitive e-mail and enforce adequate security measures to safeguard trade secrets.
- Companies should develop a plan for data recovery in case the system crashes or fails. Data back-ups should be maintained and kept safely.

3.6 E-mail

The components of an e-mail system include- user messages, sender's and recipient's addresses, protocol, messaging transports, gateways, value-added networks, and directory systems.

3.6.1 What Constitutes a Good E-Mail?

To make the Internet experience an enjoyable and pleasant one, it is important to follow certain practices known as netiquette. This is a set of rules to be adhered to while sending e-mails, chatting online or blogging.

Some rules must be observed while writing e-mails. These guidelines constitute e-mail etiquette:

- Make your mail easy to read.
- Use the subject line to tell the recipient the purpose of the message.
- Use concrete words that avoid negative connotations. Be aware of the positive and negative meanings, that is, know the denotation and connotation of the words used. For example, the word 'temporary' is a neutral one. A positive word for this would be 'alternate' and the negative 'makeshift'. Another neutral word is 'end'; the positive word is 'finished' or 'conclude' whereas the negative word is 'abandon' or 'terminate' (*Booher, 2007*).
- Use short, focused paragraphs. Each paragraph should have a topic sentence, related sentences, and transitional elements. In business writing, the topic sentence should usually come at the beginning of the paragraph.
- Quote previous e-mails when responding to questions or requests.
- You are sending e-mails within your organization, know and follow its rules for using this facility. Do not write anything in a way that could become embarrassing for you or your organization.
- Use the appropriate level of formality. If you are writing to your boss, be as formal as you are expected to be. Read your fellow employees' e-mails to inform yourself about the organization's approach.
- Write in a clear and organized manner. Use short and simple sentences. Use correct spelling and basic grammar.
- Write in the active voice mostly. For instance, instead of using the passive voice "The reports are to be submitted by the employees before 5.00 p.m.", write in the active voice as 'Please submit your reports by 5.00 pm'.
- Generally, the length of your message should be kept to one screen only. If there is a file or document you want your reader to view, send it as an attachment with your e-mail.
- Start your message with the most important information you want to exchange with or receive from the recipient.
- Use conventional rules for punctuation and capitalization.

- Be sure of the recipient's email address. A mistake in a single letter will send it to the wrong person. Check that the computer's internal clock and date settings are correct.
- Revise your draft after composing it. Use the computer's grammar and spell-checkers. If you have doubts about the content, then save it as a draft and rethink. Send only when, you are sure.

Booher, 2007.

3.6.2 Avoid the following while writing Emails

- Do not treat e-mail as casual conversation. This may lead to including comments or remarks that one would not dream of saying in person or typing in a letter, thereby creating inter-personal conflicts and tensions.
- Do not use jargon and slang. At times, technical jargon may be used when communicating with colleagues of your own profession as they would understand the terms.
- Do not send sensitive, critical/confidential company information through e-mail which may harm the company's interests.
- Do not think that just because you have deleted e-mail it has been destroyed permanently. It can still exist in the computer's hard drive and backup storage devices at both sender's and receiver's locations.
- Avoid using the 'Reply all' button unless necessary.
- While forwarding messages, write a brief note at the beginning of the forwarded message to explain why you are sending it and what action you wish the recipient to take.

3.7 E-Commerce: The Revolution

E-commerce is a commercial transaction which is mediated by digital technology. This includes the use of the Web and Internet to transact business. It may, therefore, be referred to as 'digitally enabled commercial transactions' between and among organizations and individuals. (*Laudon and Traver, 2006*).

Any commercial activity involves buyers, sellers, and producers. Buyers are those people who have the money and are interested in buying goods or services. Sellers offer goods and services to the buyers. Producers are the people who create/manufacture goods and services that sellers offer to buyers.

Before the advent of e-commerce, the process of selling and marketing of products was done through the use of sales personnel and mass marketing strategies. Consumers were lured to products through advertising campaigns that were aimed at influencing their perceptions about products and their purchasing behavior. They were also limited by geographical and social boundaries as well as insufficient information about comparative prices and quality. E-commerce has changed and challenged traditional methods of business transactions.

3.7.1 Advantages of E-Commerce

- The global reach of e-commerce is phenomenal. Commercial transactions now can cross cultural and national boundaries conveniently and cost effectively in comparison to the earlier methods of commerce.
- It is a market which is always present everywhere. It is not restricted by physical space or geographical boundaries. Hence transaction costs, that is, the cost of participating in a market, are greatly reduced.
- E-commerce follows universal standards for conducting business practice. These technical standards are followed by countries all over the world and have lowered market entry costs, that is, the amount merchants have to pay to bring their goods to the market. At the same time, costs for searching suitable products are decreased for customers.
- E-commerce technologies provide increased information density. Information density is the total amount and quality of information available to all its market participants, consumers, and merchants. The new technologies enabling e-commerce reduce information collection and storage, processing, and communication costs. They also provide more accurate and timely information. This has made prices and costs more transparent, and the consumer can find out the variety of prices prevailing in a market as well as the costs merchants have to pay for products.
- More purchases can be made with each transaction. The e- commerce company, Amazon, not only describes the books/ articles available online but also shows what other people purchased along with the book(s)/ articles had ordered. It also gives a review of the selected book(s)/products and invites more reviews of it. Features like these attract the customer to buy more than what s/he would like in a normal bookshop.
- E-commerce enables companies to create larger catalogues of their products.
- It creates better and more fruitful customer interaction. With advanced automated tools, it is possible to interact with a customer in different ways.

Laudon and Traver, 2007.

3.7.2 Communication Technologies

Groupware

1. **E-meeting systems**

Refers to software that lets people at the same or different locations share information, communicate electronically, and coordinate their efforts easily. It is designed to help people who are working together on the same project/task to achieve their purpose/goal. It is an umbrella term describing electronic technologies that support group collaboration. To illustrate with an example- Google Workspace, you can find many applications in the Google Workspace to understand how groupware can help in a collaborative task. Like the group-authoring system which allows collaborative writing between different people so that they can plan, draft, revise and track a document. This program keeps an 'edit trail' of all revisions/changes made, who made them and when. It enables a supervisor/team manager to monitor workflow. Such programs are time-effective as they reduce the need for time consuming face- to-face meetings.

Advantages of Using Groupware

Files can be shared between team members who can post files that can be viewed or downloaded individually. It helps to carry out a synchronous discussion between team members by posting comments to a discussion list. Each member can read/download these comments whenever it is convenient and even post further comments on the previous ones. The original file remains unaltered while team members attach their comments to it.

Announcements in schedules, changes, deadlines, and holidays can also be posted. Team members can be notified by e-mail alerts when a document has been changed. Better cost control and increased productivity are the main benefits of groupware. It is easier to integrate geographically disparate locations. Routine processes and tasks can be automated.

Shared Whiteboards These allow two or more people to view and draw on a shared drawing surface even from different locations as if they were all in a room. These are designed for informal conversation, but they may also support sophisticated drawing tasks such as collaborative graphic design, publishing, or engineering applications. Many computers are linked together to form a network. The users share a common whiteboard on which data/information can be modified. A person may be drawing or pointing- this is shown by tele-pointers which are color coded or labeled to identify each person. Nowadays, many such applications are in place, and we use them in our lives to make it simpler.

Video communications/Video conferencing Systems These permit two-way or multi-way calling with live video. The audio and video signals that transmit live voices and images are transmitted through different media like telephone lines, direct cable connection, but mostly through the Internet. With the advent of technological developments like social media platforms, and various connecting software, it has emerged a popular way of connecting with people.

Can you name some of these platforms and software that you actively use to connect to people in various geographical locations?

Another advantage of video conferencing is that it can also provide overviews of activities at a remote location. Video conferencing has become popular in recent years because of the increasing cost of travel, more affordable transmission cost and the invention of more effective hardware. It can also be used to share documents, computer-displayed information, and whiteboards.

Guidelines for Conducting Video Conferences

The preparation for any video conference/ meeting will be similar to organizing a meeting in physical mode. *Markel, 2004.*

- First plan and prepare an agenda ahead of the conference.
- Provide all participants with copies of agenda, handouts, visual aids, etc., ahead of time.
- Speak normally, be audible.
- Introduce yourself before speaking and wait until the camera is focused on you.

- If you wish to show graphics, prepare them with the video in mind. They should be simple with readable fonts.
- Avoid sudden movements. Do not gesture or move around unnecessarily. Maintain a quiet posture and rely more on your voice, than on your hands to convey your point.

2. **Importance of Video Conferencing in Education** It gives students an opportunity to learn by participating in a multi-way communication platform. Classes in remote and isolated places can be taught by teachers from different places. Students belonging to diverse backgrounds can come together and learn about each other's culture and ideas. Students can visit other parts of the world through 'virtual' field trips. A teacher can keep in touch with the class while attending a conference. A researcher can collaborate with colleagues at other institutions on a regular basis, thereby saving time on travel. These platforms also allow you to mark attendance, record lectures, submit assignments and participate in quizzes and exams.

Can you share your experience of using some of these platforms to attend classes during the Covid-19 pandemic time?

3. Chat Systems They allow many people to write messages in real time in a public space, thereby creating a virtual group. As each person writes a message, it can be seen at the bottom of a scrolling screen. Chat groups are formed by having listed chat rooms by name, location, number of users, topic of discussion, etc. The text version of chat is useful as it has a direct transcript of the conversation. It also allows backward referencing during conversation, making it easier for people to drop into a conversation and to pick up the threads of the ongoing discussion.

Have you ever used some of the chat systems in your online social interactions?

Decision Support Systems They facilitate groups in taking decisions. They provide tools for brainstorming, critiquing ideas, voting, etc. It is presumed that such systems aid groups to arrive at more rational and even-handed decisions. They are designed to facilitate meetings, encourage equal participation by, for instance, providing anonymity and enforcing turn taking.

3.8 Oral Business Communication

Oral communication is vital to human relationships in all business organizations, as well as in other social organizations. It is the oldest and most commonly used channel of human communication. Though it is the easiest of all modes of communication, it is the most difficult to master. The success of any organization depends to a large extent on managing both the formal and informal oral communication. Oral communication can be effective only if it is concise and informative, clear, relevant, and tactful in words and tone. Some of the various kinds of formal oral communication are: *Seeley, 2007.*

- Talking over the telephone
- How to appear and conduct interviews
- Meetings
- Group discussions
- Presentations

We will begin with the issue of how the telephone is an important mode of formal communication in an organization. The effective use of telephone saves time and money together with helping you to communicate effectively. We will then move on to talk about how to succeed and conduct interviews, the preparation required and the follow-up after facing an interview. This section will also talk about the basics of conducting an interview and how the role of the interviewer and the interviewee is important for a successful interview. Another important mode of oral communication is active participation in meetings to resolve conflicts and arrive at solutions to problems. The chapter on group discussions will talk about group discussions in organizations or as part of academic curriculum and how to participate in them effectively.

The last issue being discussed is presentations. It is one of the most important genres of oral business communication. It is a situation where one person speaks while others listen. Presentations can take place in small groups and also with a large audience. Verbal skills are very important to be a good presenter and in public speaking. We will talk about the planning, structure, and delivery of presentations in this section.

There are many advantages of oral communication. It provides immediate response and clarification from the respondent, without any time lag. Messages sent orally not only save time but also cut down paperwork and maintenance of files. Oral communication is the appropriate mode of communication if you want to take immediate action on any issue. Communicating with colleagues in meetings and over the telephone helps in understanding each other better along with building relationships. This promotes a positive and healthy working environment in an organization.

Oral communication is an effective tool of persuasion. It is much simpler and easier to resolve conflicts by talking rather than writing to each other. Communicating orally builds an environment of informality among colleagues leading to better interaction and understanding among them. It is a cost-effective device both in terms of money and time. It also has the added advantage of adapting and improving, unlike the written word which is more rigid in nature.

3.8.1 Using the Telephone

Pre-reading Activity
When do you generally use the telephone? Do you use the phone to talk about some problem? Is there a difference in your language and tone when you speak to your friend and when you speak to a person in an office? What are these differences and what are the reasons for them?

The telephone is an important channel of communication in today's fast-moving world where time is at a premium. It will continue to be an indispensable means of communication. It seems to have all the advantages of a face-to-face meeting and is also an effective management tool.

3.8.2 Advantages of Using a Telephone

One of the major advantages of using the phone is the instant reactions and instant flow of information and the consequent actions that follow it. There is no time lag in decisions being taken. Telephone, as a medium of communication has taken a huge leap forward as now, we use it for variety of purpose- from attending online classes, being connected with the friends on social media, online shopping or seeking information from the Internet- everything can be accessed from the tip of the finger. Telephone also gives us the option to record the conversation, block someone's number if you so desire, video calling using different platforms, conferencing etc.

3.8.3 Disadvantages of Using a Telephone

At times when one calls, the answering machine becomes a barrier to communication. You also have to depend entirely on voice modulation to communicate. This requires a good accent, perfect pronunciation and excellent vocabulary which may become a stumbling block for many of us. The conversation on the telephone is also dependent on the network. The possibility of cross connection and wrong number can also hinder communication. Sometimes, you may miss out or misinterpret some information which may lead to numerous other problems. It is also not easy to ascertain the appropriate time to call a person. The receiver could be in a bad mood or busy and, therefore, calling her/him would not serve the desired purpose. It means that you cannot read the non-verbal signals (an important aspect of communication) and actions of a person while making a phone call. Moreover, conversation over the phone does not provide a permanent record for legal purposes.

3.8.4 General Preparation

You should be aware of the various features of a telephone set which would enable greater efficiency. In addition to it, please ensure which is the redialling button, number display facility, retrieving voice mail, auto dialling if the line is busy and call-transfer facility. You should always keep a pen and a pad near the telephone set.

Before making a formal call keep the following points in mind:

- **Brevity and precision**- your conversation should be brief and precise.
- **Clarity**- you should speak slowly and clearly; your tone should be cheerful and your voice lively. To give out names and addresses over the phone, spell them out with familiar words to illustrate each letter. For example, if you want to spell the name Arun, then say A for Ajmer, R for Ranchi, U for Udaipur, and N for Nagpur.

3.8.5 How to Make a Call

Before making a call, you should keep in mind the appropriate time for making it. It is always good to call in the forenoon or early afternoon as people are generally available at that time. Unless you are familiar with the person you should not call his residence unless it is absolutely warranted. Also, be careful of the time you call people across a different time zone.

The purpose of the call should be clearly defined- whether it is to give or receive information or whether it is a confirmation of some issue. Make a brief note about all the points that are to be discussed before dialling the number. This will not only impress the receiver of the professionalism of the caller but will also ensure that all important points are discussed, and nothing is missed out.

- All the documents and letters concerned with the call should be kept handy in case you need to refer to them.

- When the call is answered, greet the listener, and then introduce yourself. For example, I'm Arun Kumar from Bharath Enterprises. If someone else picks up the phone, politely ask to be connected to the concerned person after a formal introduction. You must identify yourself every time a call is made because it is basic telephone etiquette.
- You must sound confident, decisive, and interested while making the call and all this has to be conveyed through your voice.
- Once the phone has been connected to the right person and pleasantries exchanged ask the person if it is the right time to call. Generally, people will listen but in case somebody would like to be spoken to later, respect her/his wishes and call her/him later at her/his convenience.
- Be brief and clear in communicating the issue. Being lucid and conveying the message in the right sequence helps in comprehension for the listener. If it is a long conversation do summarize the main points at the end before disconnecting.
- If the line is disconnected before the conversation is complete, do redial and complete the conversation.
- Do not forget to thank the person before disconnecting. Note down the decisions taken, if any, and also the dates of the meetings, after the call is over.
- If any action is required to be taken after the call, it should be done immediately lest one forgets.
- Be prepared to leave a message if the concerned person is not available. As a precaution, try to draft the message beforehand.

Lesikar and Flatley, 2002

3.9 Teleconferencing

Teleconferencing is a meeting or conference where the participants are sitting in conference rooms that are in various locations and interacting with each other using different software and platforms like G-Meet, Microsoft Teams etc. We are well familiar with these platforms as we have extensively used them during the covid-19 pandemic. During this kind of meeting, the advantage of exchanging ideas and views without physically having to move is one of the greatest merits of teleconferencing. A lot of planning and organization is required to conduct a teleconference meeting.

3.9.1 Organizing a Conference Call

All the participants should be informed of the time and date beforehand. If it is a global teleconference, then the organizers should keep the different time zones in mind while fixing the meeting. The agenda for the meeting should be circulated well in advance. All the participants must be punctual for the meeting, or else the others would keep waiting. Once everybody is connected the host should introduce everyone by name and designation. Moreover, a clear idea of how the conference will be conducted, i.e. in which order the participants will be asked to speak, should also be notified. Once the conference is over the minutes of the meeting should be mailed to every participant.

3.9.2 Participating in a Conference Call

A member should only speak when the host requests him to do so or if they have a pertinent point to make. The participants should take notes of what others are saying so that they can comprehend and respond accordingly. Every member should go through the agenda thoroughly and have all necessary information and files regarding the conference call. Participants should be brief and clear while speaking. Members should speak slowly so that others can understand, especially if there are participants from other countries. One should be a good listener, and no one should try to dominate the proceedings. Only a good listener can be a good speaker.

Soundararaj, 2007.

3.9.3 Interviews, Using Telephone, Meetings, Group Discussions, Oral Presentations, Public Speaking, Presentation Aids

3.9.3.1 Interviews

Interviews are planned interpersonal communication with a predetermined purpose. All the members participating in this activity need to prepare themselves for it. The purpose of the interview defines the exchange of information and ideas between the participants. The purpose of the interview could be hiring for employment, promotion, appraisal etc.,

An interview can also be defined as a conversation between two parties in which at least one of them has a defined and serious purpose. It can also be defined as a purposeful and meaningful exchange of ideas between two people (*Choudhary et. al, 2011*).

Given below are the different kinds of interviews one has to face in an organization.

3.9.3.2 Different Kinds of Interviews

1. **Selection/employment interviews:** This is generally conducted when a company wants to hire people in its organization.

2. **Promotion interviews:** It is held when an employee wants to be considered for a higher position in the organization.

3. **Appraisal interviews:** This is conducted either periodically or annually by the organization to evaluate the performance of the employees and to review the progress or discuss the future course of action of the organization.

4. **Counseling interviews:** They are conducted to help employees who are facing problems in the workplace or on the personal front, and at times, if the performance of the employees is not up to the desired level.

5. **Disciplinary/reprimand interviews:** When an employee breaks the code of conduct, breaches the rules of the company, or does not maintain discipline of the organization he is summoned and reprimanded by the employer for his undesirable behavior.

6. **Grievance interviews:** These interviews are conducted by the organization to ascertain if an employee has a complaint either against the organization or his senior or junior colleagues.

7. **Exit interviews:** Such an interview takes place when an employee is leaving an organization either voluntarily or through dismissal. The idea behind conducting this interview is that an employee who is leaving will be forthright and open in his comments about the organization, which will help the organization to take corrective measures to improve itself.

8. **Stay interview:** This is a fairly new phenomenon, and companies are using it to judge employees' 'expectation' and it helps them to retain their workforce by making the employees feel appreciated and motivated.

Interviews are also conducted to measure the satisfaction, the working conditions of the employees, their attitudes and other issues related to creating a healthy and positive environment for them to work in. *Monippally, 2001.*

3.9.3.3 Different Kinds of Interview Strategies

1. **Depth or action interviews**: These are specialized interviews where interpersonal communication takes place to find out the personal interests of the interviewee. The questions generally asked are concerned with the family, education, interests and hobbies and the aptitude of the candidate. The rationale of this kind of an interview is that helps in understanding the person as an individual apart from his other qualifications.

2. **Group or discussion interviews:** In this kind of an interview, several candidates join simultaneously to see how they interact with each other. This kind of an interview helps in judging interpersonal skills of individuals.

3. **Stress interview:** This strategy helps to gauge how well a person handles stressful situations. The interviewer assumes a hostile approach towards the candidates. They are asked pointed questions designed to irk, embarrass, or unsettle them. They may be subjected to criticism in the way they dress or present themselves, deliberate interruptions, long periods of silence, abrupt and, at times, hostile reactions of the interviewer. The idea is to find out how a person functions under stressful conditions, and his capability to handle a crisis.

4. **Situational interview:** In this kind of an interview, the interviewer gives a situation and asks the candidate how he would deal with it. People who support this approach believe such an interview creates a real-life situation between an employer who needs a job to be done and a worker who must be fully prepared to execute it.

5. **Video interviews:** Many employers use this method to cut down on the cost of travel and wastage of time while travelling to the organization by the candidates. This has emerged as a popular medium nowadays post the pandemic. One needs to prepare differently as compared to a face-to-face interview.

3.9.3.4 How to Face an Interview

An interviewee needs to prepare on a number of fronts before the interview. Nowadays, having the right kind of personality is important for getting selected for a particular job. A number of companies are now looking for what is called high EQ (emotional quotient). Candidates with high EQ possess certain attributes like self-awareness, good impulse control, persistence, confidence, motivation, good interpersonal skills, persuasion powers and articulation.

What's Your EQ?

- *Think clearly and stay focused on the task at hand while under pressure. Admit your own mistakes.*
- *Meet commitments and keep promises. Hold yourself accountable for meeting your goals. Seek new ideas from a variety of sources.*
- *Handle multiple demands and changing priorities.*
- *Make sacrifices to meet an important organizational goal.*
- *Cut through red tape and bend outdated rules when necessary.*
- *Seek fresh perspectives, even if that means trying something totally new.*
- *Operate from an expectation of success rather than a fear of failure.*
- *Try to leam how to improve your performance. Set challenging goals and take calculated risks to reach them. (Bovee et al, 2006)*

For a successful interview, preparation is mandatory. The best way to prepare for a job interview is to think about the job itself and then prepare. There are certain things that one needs to prepare before facing the interview board.

3.9.3.5 Before the Interview

Gather information about the organization and if possible, about the members of the interview board. Newspapers, journals, business periodicals and the Internet will give enough information about the organization, its operations, its market, its strategies, and its financial status.

Anticipate the questions that the interviewer may ask on the basis of your cv/ biodata and the job requirement and rehearse the answers.

You can also prepare a list of questions which you may like to ask the interviewer. Do keep in mind the fact that asking relevant questions is as important as giving relevant answers.

Prepare yourself with mock interviews and try to polish your interview style to create the right impact at the interview. Pay special attention to nonverbal behavior while facing the interview board. Always maintain eye contact, sit attentively and be pleasant yet not servile in your behavior. These gestures convey that you are alert, confident, responsible, and energetic. Any cultural differences of the organization you plan to join should be kept in mind so that no one is offended by your behavior.

It is important to look good and presentable in front of the interview board. A positive impression initially helps to create a positive attitude amongst the members of the interview board. The clothes, shoes, and accessories you wear should not only be comfortable but also appropriate and acceptable.

Put all your credentials in a neat file and carry a set of spare copies.

Arrive at the venue a little before time so that you can familiarize yourself with the environment and be relaxed. *Monippally, 2001.*

3.9.3.6 During the Interview

- Enter the room with a confident smile and greet the member/members appropriately.
- Take a seat only when asked to do so.
- Do not be fidgety or nervous. Maintain a calm and composed posture.
- Do not lean on the table or sit with your hands on the table.
- Use appropriate and positive body language- neither too stiff nor too casual.
- Be a careful listener and listen to the questions carefully before responding.

- All the questions need to be answered carefully and completely. Be straight forward in your answers.
- If you do not know the answers say so to the interview board politely.
- Avoid talking too much or being boastful about your achievements. It is important to prove your worth by action not words.
- Use correct expressions and language which is suitable to the occasion. Avoid using incomplete sentences and phrases when responding. There should be clarity both in speech and thought.
- Be honest and open about your previous employer and job.
- When given an opportunity to ask questions, do so but ask questions about their expectations from you, your responsibilities, and the future potential of the organization, among other things. Asking questions about salary, holidays and other benefits leaves a negative impression on the interviewer's mind.
- Bid a polite farewell. Thank them for considering you for the job. You can conclude with a positive 'forward-looking' statement about your potential role in the company.

Seeley, 2007.

3.9.3.7 After the Interview

- Send a 'thank you' note within two days of the interview. This gives the impression that you are keenly motivated to take up the job and the interview board is forced to remember you which may work in your favor.
- If you do not receive any response within the promised time, write a letter to enquire about the results. A good interview is one in which all the people participating in it are actively involved.

3.10 Meetings

Pre-reading Activity

- Have you attended any meeting- Students' Union Meeting, Mess Secretary Meeting or GBM of the Students' Council or the Senate?
- Do you find it easy or difficult to participate in these meetings? Why?
- Why do you think meetings are called in an organization?
- Is it important to follow certain rules and regulations while conducting or participating in a meeting?

Meetings are an effective and efficient tool in the process of communication. This helps in allowing people to meet each other and at the same time it helps them to share information and ideas, make relevant suggestions, take quick decisions, and consequently facilitate the efficient working of the organization. Meetings can be called for several reasons. Some of them are listed below:

- To generate ideas and discussion on a particular issue
- To report on some decision taken
- To communicate some important information to people
- To get people involved in the decision-making process
- To elicit opinion and assistance on certain issues
- To reconcile conflicting views
- To create new ideas
- To evaluate the performance of the organization

Meetings also help in enhancing the social skills of the group. The participants can exchange and share information about issues not related to the office. Sometimes, meetings focus specifically on the issues of working together and celebrating achievements. This enables the members of the group to come closer and helps in improving the performance of the group. A meeting should be called not because it is the option available by default but only to achieve an objective in a specific situation.

3.10.1 Types of Meeting

There are generally two kinds of meetings formal meetings and informal meetings. Formal meetings need to be conducted according to certain rules and regulations as laid down in their constitution or any other formal document. Certain requirements have to be fulfilled to validate a meeting which is also called parliamentary procedure, they are:

- Agenda to be circulated beforehand.
- Quorum must be complete.
- Formal records of minutes to be maintained.

Some formal meetings held by an organization are:

- Annual general meeting
- Statutory meeting
- Board meeting

Some informal meetings held by an organization are:

- Departmental meeting
- Inter-departmental meetings
- Working parties

3.10.2 Planning the Meeting

Sometimes, people are not clear why a meeting is being held. To keep expectation in line with reality, 'Purpose Process Outcomes' design can be followed to plan meetings.
Purpose: Inform participants ahead of time about the meeting's purpose.
Is the meeting informative?
Are participants making decisions? Is it a brainstorming session?
Is it a planning meeting?

Process: Give an overview of the plans and expectations of what will be accomplished.
How will the meeting be conducted?
For decisions, do participants need to reach a consensus?
Does the majority rule, or does the leader determine the outcome based on the group's input?

Outcome: Identify the meeting's intended outcomes
What is in it for the participants?
What will participants walk away with?
What results do we expect?

The purpose and process can be conveyed in the agenda that is sent out to announce the meeting. The items on the agenda should follow a logical order. If there are certain items on the agenda which require information or facts to be circulated, then it should be done well in advance. Only the relevant people should be invited to the meeting otherwise it would be very difficult to control and conduct the meeting as well as achieve the goal for which it was convened.

3.10.3 Role of the Convener/Chairperson

The chairperson needs to follow certain conventions and traditions for the meeting to run smoothly. First and foremost, the chairperson should arrive on time. Punctuality by the chairperson sets the tone for the successful conduct of the meeting.

- One should not wait for the latecomers; however important they may be for the group.

- Although the agenda has already been circulated, it is a good idea for the chairperson to redefine the agenda for the benefit of those who may not have gone through it earlier.
- If the meeting is started on a positive note all the members feel comfortable and relaxed and can contribute fruitfully to the meeting.
- It is advisable for the chairperson to be a patient and active listener and impartially control the proceedings of the meeting.
- Sometimes, heated discussions or arguments may erupt among the members. The chairperson has a very crucial role to play at this juncture. Not only is he required to sort out the problem amicably, but also be impartial yet firm in his dealings.
- The chairperson should follow the agenda strictly and if any member strays from it, it is the duty of the chairperson to bring the meeting back on track without offending anyone.
- Any issue which is not on the agenda can be discussed at the end of the meeting with the permission of the chair or postponed for a further meeting.
- The items on the agenda should be taken up serially because they have been arranged in a logical order. Though all the items should be discussed in complete detail, repetition and unwarranted comments should be avoided.
- After each item has been discussed, the chairperson should summarize the decision of the group both for clarity and to avoid any misinterpretation or miscommunication.
- At the end of the meeting all the decisions taken should be summarized, though the minutes of the meeting will formally provide the summary. Summarizing all the decisions taken also gives a feeling of achievement to the members.
- A meeting should be concluded on time. This reflects the efficiency and professionalism of the chairperson.

Taylor, 2005.

3.10.4 How to Participate in a Meeting

The responsibility of a participant is as important as that of the chairman for the smooth functioning of the meeting. The participants need to observe certain etiquette to help the meeting run efficiently. Here are a few guidelines:

- Be punctual Do not interrupt other speakers.
- Be a receptive listener.

- Do not dominate the meeting.
- Do not deviate from the agenda.
- Do not disobey the chair, cooperate with the chair.
- Do not joke, laugh, or make irrelevant comments.
- Do not talk over the phone during the meeting.

Members attending a meeting must make some positive contribution to the meeting and not be a mere number needed to complete the quorum. The contribution of the members will depend entirely on how well-prepared s/he is and how s/he conducts himself in the meeting.

Be familiar with the agenda. If there is a need, gather more information and data regarding any particular issue. Be a good and active listener. It is important to be receptive to other people's ideas and opinions before giving your own views on any issue. Choose an appropriate time to voice your opinion so that it has an impact.

Always keep a pen and paper at hand to note down any point or fact which seems relevant or needs to be discussed in detail.

3.10.5 Factors That Render Meetings Wasteful

Sometimes, meetings end with no concrete decisions taken and the whole exercise seems to have been a waste of time and energy. There are many reasons that lead to meetings being wasteful.

- Poor preparation by conveners and attendees.
- Failure to maintain and follow up minutes.
- Incompetent chairpersons who let meetings drift Cunning chairpersons who use meetings to.
- Bosses who discourage dissent at meetings delay decision-making.

3.11 Group Discussions

Pre-reading Activity

- What do you understand by a group?
- Do you discuss certain issues among your friends?
- How important is it to be open to the viewpoints of your friends?
- Is there only one solution to the issue being discussed?

A group is a unit of two or more people who work together to achieve a common goal. A group is a collection of individuals, where the members accept a common task, become interdependent in their performance, and interact with one another to promote its accomplishments." (*Kulkarni, 2006*)

Group Discussion

Before getting on with group discussions, the 3Ps which constitute the ingredients of any discussion need to be understood, namely, **Purpose, Planning and Participation.**

The members of the group should be clear about of the objective of the group discussion. The group discussion needs to be planned well, deciding on what the participants plan to discuss, and how they propose to do so.

Before we go further let us understand the pre-requisites for an effective group discussion:

Every member should be informed about the agenda, the date, time, and place of the group discussion. "A group discussion itself means that all the members are expected to participate actively in it and contribute positively to achieve the goal. A group discussion can run smoothly only if one of the members is made the team leader or group leader. It is his responsibility to ensure that the discussion moves in the right direction, and every member participates in it. The ambience of group discussions is generally informal which puts everybody at ease so that they can speak up to resolve the issue" (*Sinha, 2001*).

3.11.1 Why Decisions Made in Groups are Better than Individual Decisions

One of the most important reasons why decisions made by groups is better than individual decisions is the range of experience, variety of opinion, development of new ideas and a thorough probing of the problem by a group, which is difficult to be done by an individual.

Moreover, a decision taken by a group is readily acceptable to everybody in an organization because people from different departments participate in the decision-making process. It is also easier to coordinate, plan and execute the decision in different departments. Decisions taken by groups also ensure that the interest of the employees is safeguarded. Sometimes, a group is appointed to avoid any action to take place or even postpone a decision indefinitely.

Any decision taken by a group is easier to implement because it is the people who have taken a decision, and they feel it is their responsibility to adhere to it. It is not a decision imposed by an individual and so there is no resistance from the people.

But the whole process is very time-consuming and expensive. Many times, no concrete decision is taken because of diverse ideas and views leading to a state of indecision.

The responsibility for a decision taken is also shared by all the members of the group, and it is difficult to make any one person accountable for the final decision. There is also a possibility that some members with a hidden agenda can hijack the decision-making process to their advantage. Despite these drawbacks, a decision made by a group is always better than a decision taken by an individual and, as the saying goes, two heads are better than one. *Taylor, 2005.*

3.11.2 Participating in Group Discussions

Role of the group leader/team leader
Role of the participants

3.11.3 Role of the Group Leader

The group leader has an important and dynamic role to play to make the group an effective instrument and to take unprejudiced decisions. S/he must plan the meeting well, defining the purpose and the agenda to the members, encourage every member to participate, and moderate. A group leader also must summarize every member's view to arrive at a common consensus on the decision to be taken. Reconciling the differences between members amicably yet firmly is also the responsibility of a group leader. S/he ensures everybody observes the decorum of interaction and should be seen as impartial in her/his observations. Coordinate the discussion by giving clarification on any issue and help in arriving at a decision. Suggest creative strategies to arrive at a decision.

3.11.4 Role of the Participants

- Communicate positively to facilitate decision-making.
- It is important to be well-informed to contribute to the discussion.
- Be a good listener and open to the ideas and views of other members.
- Rigidity is never a positive trait in a group.
- Analyze coherently and argue positively to convince the other members.
- To be cordial while interacting. A hostile attitude may deter people from.
- Keep a pen and paper to note down other people's views.
- Do not monopolize the proceedings. Allow everybody to talk.
- Do not bully people to come to a consensus on any issue.

3.11.5 Here are a few traits that you need to develop or possess to be successful in group discussions

Flexibility: Do not be rigid and self-opinionated. Listen to the opinions and ideas of others, show willingness to change stand to reach a consensus.

Assertiveness: Put forward your point with clarity and conviction. Be emphatic and positive in your approach. Do not be aggressive because it is a negative quality.

Initiative: Do so if you know the subject well.

Creativity: Try to give a new perspective to the discussion, do it confidently and coherently. Help others to express their views and ideas if they are not getting an opportunity to do so.

A good listener- Listen carefully to other people, this will help to improve your own ideas. Make necessary amendments if there are faults/flaws in your ideas.

Awareness: Be aware of all the current issues and topics.

Communication skills: Have good communication skills.

3.12 Oral Presentation

Pre-reading Activity

- Have you made oral presentations like a speech, or read an article or essay in school?
- How did you prepare for it?
- Do you know what is public speaking?
- Do you think making oral presentations in formal or informal situations varies? If so, how?

Presentation- A Mode of Communication

Presentation is a mode of communication where you share information is shared live with the audience, to achieve a certain objective. Presentations are made in the following situations:

- In a seminar/or a conference.
- To introduce a new product or service.
- To present a new business plan/alternative business plan.
- To market/increase sales of a product.
- To give a briefing/information on any issue.
- To analyze a report or project.

We have to acquire certain skills to be a good presenter, namely,

- Skill of condensed writing.
- Skill of structuring and organizing notes.
- Skill of public speaking.

3.12.1 There are four types of presentations:

- Impromptu presentation
- Extempore presentation
- Scripted presentation
- Memorized presentation.

But generally, when we talk of oral presentations we are referring to scripted and extempore presentation.

3.12.2 Advantage of Oral Presentation

An oral presentation has certain advantages over a written presentation.
First, it allows dialogue between the presenter and his audience.
Second, the audience is free to ask questions, make comments or clarify any issue.
Third, the presenter and the audience have the liberty to talk before, between and after the presentation.
Any presentation has three basic elements: namely, the presenter, the audience, and the su3bject matter.

3.12.3 Features of a Good Presentation

1. **Purpose:** The purpose of the presentation should be clear in our mind. The presentation may be given-
   - To sell a product.
   - To make people aware about the issue.
   - To give information about a product/service/problem/proposal.
   - To discuss and debate upon a business proposal.
   - To persuade people on an issue.
   - To motivate people to improve work culture.

2. To **assess** the audience and the contents accordingly. It is important to know the level of the audience and if the contents match the audience's expectation. The presentation will not succeed if the idea put across is too simple or too difficult to communicate. Moreover, the contents should not be boring and irrelevant for the audience. The language used in the presentation should be simple and comprehensible. In effect, the expectation of the audience should be met in content and language. For example, if we have to make a presentation on the Pandemic-covid-19 to a group of science students, and a group of illiterate laborers, obviously

the presentation will be different for these two groups though the topic will remain the same.

3. **Brevity:** A good presentation should be brief. Generally, one is given 30 minutes to make a presentation at a professional platform.

4. **Attitude of audience:** It is important to gauge the attitude of the audience towards the topic of the presentation- interested, unconcerned, hostile, or open minded.

5. **Ideas and information sequenced well:** A good presentation should have a coherent sequence of both ideas and visuals to have the desired effect. If it is not so, the presentation will confuse the audience, leaving them dissatisfied and bored.

6. **Use of other modes to make an effective presentation:** Statistical data, visual aids and case illustrations help to make the presentation informative and interesting

7. **Delivery:** The presentation should be made lively and interesting. A confident and enthusiastic presenter is in constant dialogue with the audience while making the presentation. Maintaining eye contact with the audience together with appropriate body gestures and voice modulation will add in making a positive impact of the presentation.

8. **Humour** is an important ingredient in any presentation. If you perceive that the audience is hostile, the best way to disarm them is to add humour to your presentation. A small dose of humour in the presentation makes it interesting and holds the attention of the audience.

Soundararaj, 2007.

3.12.4 Planning the Presentation

A presentation requires a lot of preparation before it takes a final shape. Depending on the focus of the presentation, you decide the strategy or sequence of ideas. *Sinha, 2005.*

3.12.5 Who, Why, Where, When, What

The presentation prepared by us goes through the five filters of who, why, where, when, and what before it takes a final shape. These five filters help to polish the presentation before it is ready for the audience.

Who: This focuses on 'who the target audience is; what is their complete profile- age, gender, literacy level, the language they understand, their attitudes, comprehension levels, their values and constraints, political affiliations, etc. Knowing and understanding these issues will help one to communicate better with them. The other point to consider is 'who' you are to them: boss, colleague, a professional, an expert or a nobody. One needs to blend both the who's to make an effective presentation.

Why: This is the second filter. You need to answer the question as to why you are making the presentation. What is the objective and what do you hope to achieve? Is it to persuade the audience, motivate them, educate them, convince them, or give some information on an issue? The other point which needs to be answered is why is the audience there and what do they hope to get from the presentation?

Where: The next issue is where will the presentation take place? Will it be in a classroom, conference hall, or a seminar room? Does it have all the facilities that one requires to make the presentation such as a computer, projector, and an Internet connection?

When: It is important to know when your presentation will take place. Are there people who have already made presentations before you and discussed some of the issues? To hold the interest of the audience, avoid repetition and adapt accordingly. There could also be a paucity of time, so one must know what to present and what to leave out without any negative impact on the presentation.

Finally, the most important part of the preparation is the **what** of the presentation. Here, one must be clear about the content of the presentation, namely, what are the issues that will hold the interest of the audience, how important is it to go into minute detailing, and what are the different kinds of visual aids required to support the presentation? While preparing notes for the presentation, be clear as to what you must give them what you ought to give them and what you may give them. This will help you to adapt your presentation accordingly and save you from last-minute chaos and confusion.

3.12.6 Structure of the Presentation

Every presentation has a classical structure that includes the following parts:
Introduction: Introduce the topic, its purpose and relevance.
Ensure that the topic is relevant for the audience.
Ask questions to the audience. Focus on content and concept.

Body: Break content into two or three major points.
Give evidence of content with relevant examples. Answer questions raised in the introduction.
Discuss main points thoroughly.

Conclusion: Sum up the issues raised in introduction and body. Summarize the major points.
Clarify doubts. Discuss the follow up action. (Young 2006)

1. **Introduction**

An introduction to the presentation needs to be imaginative and interesting to get the audience to listen to it. You can begin in any one of the following ways:

- A startling question
- A rhetorical question
- A provocative quote
- An interesting anecdote
- An exceptional joke
- The statement of a relevant problem
- A description of the topic's importance to the audience
- A piece of statistical information
- A summary statement of the structure
- Definition of the purpose of the presentation.

(*Monippally, 2001*)

2. **Body**

You need to define the scope of the presentation to yourself and decide what will go into it together with the sequence which should be followed. Both these issues can be taken care of if you have the answers to who, why, where and when of the sequencing of ideas needs to be logical. It is not a bad idea to first give the more acceptable ideas to the audience, thus putting them into a more positive frame of mind and then give the not so acceptable ideas which may then be accepted readily.

3. **Conclusion** This holds as important a place as the other two. It is a good idea to summarize the main points here and to tie any loose ends which you may have left while making the presentation.

- Do not end abruptly because of shortage of time.
- Do not be presumptuous.
- Tell the audience that you have delivered what you had promised in your introduction.
- Do not be tentative or self-doubting.
- Avoid long conclusions. Make a statement of the main message in strong language in the conclusion.
- End the speech on a climatic note.

3.12.7 How to Deliver the Presentation- An Art of Public Speaking

Whichever method we decide to deliver a presentation, it is important to rehearse it at least a couple of times. One is then confident, knows well the matter to be delivered, and there are no embarrassing fumbles during the presentation. It is important to decide the method of presentation. There are generally three methods:

- **Reading**
- **Memorizing**
- **Extempore/speaking from notes**

1. Reading

The advantage of using this method is that the content is before you, and the chance of missing any of the issues will be rare. But the disadvantage is that you would be so concerned about reading each word that the other issues of a presentation will get neglected. You may sound too formal and as you are concentrating on each word there will be no eye contact with the audience and the delivery can become very monotonous, which may put off the audience. You may miss punctuation marks, fumble on certain words, and lose control of the situation. It is advisable to read a presentation in very formal situations; otherwise, an interactive method is the best.

2. Memorizing

Memorizing a speech and then delivering it is an art which everyone is not adept at. Moreover, when you memorize a speech, you memorize the words rather than the meanings. If by mistake you forget some words or get stuck somewhere, it will be very difficult to continue after that. You may miss some words, get confused and consequently start panicking which will ruin the presentations. You are wholly concentrating on trying to remember rather than trying to present, you will not interact with the audience at all. People may not be impressed with this kind of presentation.

3. Extempore/Speaking from Notes

This is by far the most effective and popularly acceptable method of delivering the presentation. You can carry a few cards or notes with the main ideas written on them. The complete outline is there in your mind, the notes help to fill in the details if required. This kind of a presentation sounds natural, convincing and you can connect with the audience. Though the situation is formal you can make the presentation informal by your style and delivery and get the audience to listen carefully and respond appropriately. The spontaneity in this kind of a presentation has a positive impact on people. The ease of delivery gives the impression that you know the subject and have prepared well for the presentation.

There are other issues that you need to keep in mind while making a presentation.

Your posture and dress are important. You should stand straight, be comfortable and confident, and dress appropriately. Your facial expressions and body language should be confident and enthusiastic and give the impression that you are enjoying the presentation as much as the audience. It is important to make eye contact with the audience. This kind of nonverbal communication involves the audience in the presentation. The voice should be loud and clear and pay attention to pronunciation, speed, and voice modulation. *Business English, 2011.*

3.12.8 Using Technology and Other Mediums to Support the Presentation

To help people remember what you have said, use some visual aids to support the presentation. People may forget the spoken word but rarely forget something they have seen. Some of the visual aids that can be used are:

- **White Board-** It is used to write important words, sentences or make diagrams. It is a reliab1le aid but since all this has to be done while making the presentation, one loses precious time meant for the presentation.
- **Charts-** It has an advantage because it can be prepared in advance. It is effective for small groups but ineffective in large groups.
- **Computers and Multimedia-** By far the most popular mode of presentation nowadays. Make a PowerPoint presentation. The audience is exposed both to the spoken word and the written word. It is one of the most effective visual aids in a presentation, and
- **Models and Real Objects-** It is an excellent visual aid. The audience can see and feel it and so it has a greater impact.

3.12.9 Handling the Question-and-Answer Session

This session is an important part in public speaking or in presentation. Questions asked by the audience give you verbal feedback of the presentation and it gives you an opportunity to reemphasize your points and to clarify any doubts or misunderstandings of the audience. But it is very important to tackle the questions properly. If you are not able to satisfy the queries of the audience, it may reflect your incompetence and your credibility can be at stake. Lay down the ground rules of this session at the beginning. This will help you to have control of the session. When responding to questions repeat them for everybody's benefit, before answering. This will also help in not having to answer the same question again.

Business English, 2011.

Checklist:

- Creating Effective Slides
- Use one to two slides per minute for the presentation and four to five points per slide.
- Write effective titles.
- Be consistent with headings and subheadings.
- Do not overload the slide with information.
- Use key words and phrases. Highlight the major points.
- Avoid repetition of words and phrases.
- Use graphs rather than figures and words. Proofread your visual aids for spelling mistakes.
- Choose a readable font not a decorative one. Use color to serve a function not to decorate.
- Use animation and sound effects only if required.
- Maintain a consistency in the design of the slide.
- If you do not understand a question, seek a clarification, or rephrase it before responding to it.
- Hostile or irrelevant questions from the audience should be handled with patience or a dash of humour.
- Avoid arguments or counter questions. If the audience is not enthusiastic or too timid to ask questions, motivate them to do so.

Handling this session is an art, things can get out of control. Do not panic and be calm.

Unit Summary

In this chapter you have learnt

- *The need and purpose of an oral presentation*
- *The importance of planning, organization, and delivery of an oral presentation*
- *The advantages of using the telephone*
- *How to make and receive calls*
- *The etiquette required to make and receive calls*
- *To organize and participate in teleconferencing*
- *Groupware: different kinds- Advantages and Relevance*
- *The need for group discussions and how to be successful in group discussions*
- *The different reasons for calling a meeting*

- *The difference between formal and informal meetings*
- *How to plan a meeting*
- *The role of the chairperson in a meeting the role of other members in the meeting*
- *Different kinds of interviews are needed to test various abilities and fulfill specific needs.*
- *Varying interview strategies are required to understand and analyse individual's needs.*
- *An interviewee needs to prepare herself before, during and after the interview.*
- *It is important to know your EQ, to assess and analyze yourself.*

Exercises

Multiple Choice Questions

1. Which of the following is not one of the 7 Cs of Communication?
   a. Clarity
   b. Comprehensiveness
   c. Creativity
   d. Correctness

2. Select the correct statement:
   a. The World Wide Web (WWW) is a part of the Internet.
   b. The Internet is a part of the World Wide Web.
   c. The Internet and the World Wide Web both are one and the same thing.
   d. The World Wide Web and the Internet are not related to each other.

3. Which of the following is NOT a form of formal oral communication?
   a. Telephone conversations
   b. Group discussions
   c. Sending emails
   d. Presentations

4. The advantage of teleconferencing includes:
   a. Physical movement is required
   b. Limited interaction among participants
   c. Exchanging ideas without being physically present
   d. No planning required

5. When making a call, it is important to be mindful of:
   a. Time zones
   b. Weather conditions
   c. Traffic congestion
   d. Social media updates

6. Which one of the following is not the purpose of a presentation
   a. To make people attend a meeting.
   b. To give information about a product/service/problem/proposal.
   c. To discuss and debate upon a business proposal.
   d. To persuade people on an issue.

7. The purpose of the call should be __________ before dialing the number.
   a. Known
   b. clearly defined
   c. depends on the recipient of the call
   d. none of these

8. Oral communication is an effective tool of persuasion. (True/False)

9. During a teleconference meeting, all participants should be __________ for the meeting.
   a. Present
   b. punctual
   c. remotely present
   d. all of them

10. Of the following options, which one is not a reason to organise a meeting?
    a. To get people involved in the decision-making process
    b. To elicit opinion and assistance on certain issues
    c. To reconcile conflicting views
    d. To give a lecture on teleconferencing process

Answers: 1-c, 2-a, 3-c, 4-c, 5-a, 6-a, 7-c, 8- True, 9-d, 10-d

Subjective Questions

1. Differentiate between the Internet and the World Wide Web (WWW).
2. Differentiate between Domain Name System (DNS) and Uniform Resource Locator (URL) in the context of Internet communication.
3. What is the significance of the Internet in today's information-rich era?
4. Write an essay on the evolution of communication with the advent of the Internet and the World Wide Web.
5. Comment on the role of social media in shaping contemporary communication strategies for businesses. Discuss the advantages and disadvantages of using social media platforms for business communication.
6. Write an essay on the role and importance of manners and etiquette in e-correspondence.
7. Imagine a unique situation where the principles of effective communication are not followed. Describe the situation and its consequences.
8. Explain the importance of being a good listener in oral communication.
9. Create a dialogue between two colleagues discussing the advantages and challenges of teleconferencing in their workplace. Include their perspectives on how teleconferencing has impacted their communication and collaboration within the organization.
10. Reflect on a personal experience where oral communication played a crucial role in resolving a conflict or achieving a successful outcome. Discuss the strategies you used to communicate effectively, and the lessons learned from the experience.

KNOW MORE

- *The first e-mail was sent by Ray Tomilson in 1971. He is also credited for selecting the "@" sign to link the username with the destination address. This simple choice had a significant influence on how we now interact online.*
- *Clarity, conciseness, concreteness, correctness, coherence, completeness, and courtesy are the seven Cs of communication made prominent in the 1950s by Scott M. Cutlip and Allen H. Center in their book "Effective Public Relations."*
- *Since ancient times, conciseness has been seen as a valuable communication characteristic. The Roman Emperor Augustus was known for his condensed but impactful speeches, demonstrating the age-old significance of concise communication.*

- *In addition to being essential in the workplace, effective communication has been associated with enhanced cognitive abilities and a decreased chance of dementia in later life. Frequent, unambiguous communication stimulates the brain and keeps it mentally alert.*
- *Since it is simpler for people to comprehend than the passive voice, the active voice is often used in corporate communication. This preference stems from the directness and clarity that the active voice offers.*
- *"LO" was the first message ever transmitted via the ARPANET, the network that preceded the internet. Though the intended message was "Log in," the system collapsed after the first two characters, marking a significant turning point in the development of digital communication.*
- *While often known as "the Internet," it is essential to note that the World Wide Web is only a single application inside the broader Internet. For example, e-mail existed before the World Wide Web for almost 20 years, illustrating the resilience and longevity of Internet-based communication.*
- *Extranets facilitate collaboration across several firms, whereas intranets are designed explicitly for internal organisational communication. Extranets play a significant role in supervising supply chains and other inter-organisational processes.*
- *Mosaic was the first graphical web browser. It was introduced in 1993. Mosaic played a vital role in increasing public awareness of the World Wide Web and establishing the foundation for the rapid expansion of the Internet.*
- *The term "SPAM" refers to uninvited messages. This concept originated from a Monty Python comedy routine in which the word "SPAM" was constantly sung to symbolise unwanted and repetitious e-mails. Dealing with unwanted e-mails may be difficult, as shown by this entertaining story.*

References and Suggested Readings

Baude, D. M. (2006). *The Executive Guide to E-mail Correspondence: Including Model Letters for Every Situation*. Red Wheel/Weiser.

Comer, D. E. (2018). *The Internet book: everything you need to know about computer networking and how the Internet works*. Chapman and Hall/CRC.

Whittaker, J. (2002). *The internet: the basics*. Routledge.

Dynamic QR Coding for Further Reading

7 C's of Communication

Internet v/s World Wide Web.

Internet Terminologies

E mail etiquettes

Video Conferencing

Organisation of a Conference call

Tips for interview

Group Discussion

Tips for Oral Presentations

4 Planning and Preparing Documents for Technical Communication

Unit Specifics

An effective technical communication is accurate, clear, concise, coherent, and appropriate. But how to compose a written piece which has these qualities? There is a through planning involved in preparing them. Let us examine one by one how to achieve the above qualities in writing a document. This unit further deals with understanding the uses and importance of punctuation marks in preparing a document. To make a document effective, the appropriate use of punctuation marks plays a very important role in deriving the meaning of a sentence. In the process, you will also learn about how to make citations and give references of documents/texts/book etc. This unit also talks about planning and preparing proposals and reports, which are important components of proposing, presenting and documenting any research/ technical findings.

Apart from this at the end of the unit, a succinct recapitulation of the overall broad concepts is provided in form of a unit summary. Besides, a large number of multiple-choice questions as well as descriptive type questions are included. A list of references and suggested readings are given in the unit so that one can go through them for practice. It is important to note that for getting more information on various topics of interest some QR codes have been provided in different sections which can be scanned for relevant and supportive knowledge.

Rationale

In the last three units you have learnt about different kinds of communication, verbal-nonverbal, external-internal communication and with that you have also learnt about different kinds of communication supported by the Internet and the telecom facility. With each of them, one thing which is common is to plan and prepare a message- prepare it in such a way that it is effective to communicate and comprehend. Therefore, this unit is designed to understand the process of planning and preparing formal/organizational/official documents like proposals and reports for informational and analytical purposes. You will also learn to construct a well composed paragraph and use punctuation marks for creating effective and meaningful sentences. Reports and proposals help in various organizational activities, like decision-making, problem-solving, performance monitoring and market surveys by making these processes more thorough and well-structured. Furthermore, while planning to prepare a formal document, it is important to understand the process of citing a reference. Let's learn all of them in this unit.

Pre-requisite

Before reading this unit, the students are advised to revisit the following:

Employability Skills Class XII, Chapter 1 Communication Skills, NCERT

Basic Idea of grammatical rules and structure of English language

Basic reading of Unit I, II, III of this book

Unit Outcomes

After studying this unit, students will be able to:

U4-O1: *Understand the role and purpose of planning and preparing a document.*

U4-O2: *Differentiate between different punctuation signs and composing effective paragraphs.*

U4-O3: *Appreciate the importance of writing references and citations.*

U4-O4: *prepare short and long reports.*

U4-O5: *Identify and avoid common errors in report writing to ensure accuracy and clarity.*

U4-O6: *Develop long reports with formal elements including title pages, transmittal letters, tables of contents, and appendices.*

U4-O7: *Use effective research methods to gather and analyse data for well-structured reports.*

Unit-4 Outcomes	EXPECTED MAPPING WITH COURSE OUTCOMES *(1- Weak Correlation; 2- Medium correlation; 3- Strong Correlation)*					
	CO-1	CO-2	CO-3	CO-4	CO-5	CO-6
U4-O1	1	2	2	1	1	1
U4-O2	1	3	2	1	1	1
U4-O3	1	3	2	1	1	1
U4-O4	1	3	2	1	1	1
U4-O5	1	3	2	1	1	1
U4-O6	1	3	2	1	1	1
U4-O7	2	3	2	1	1	1

4.1 What is Planning Documents?

The preparation of any document goes through the following phases:

Understanding the nature of problem/s or the task at hand- collecting appropriate materials for writing- preparing the draft- revising the draft- proofreading.

The first and the most important stage after you have understood the nature of the problem and have completed the collection and reading of materials, is to compose a problem statement and write the introduction of the work. Thereafter comes the body of the work. This is the part where all the conceptual and practical information will be included. After you have collected your information, identified your document's purpose, objective, and outline, you are ready to start writing the first draft of your document.

While writing this part, you should pay attention to the following:

Accuracy It is necessary for a document/ draft/ manuscript to be accurate. It should be stylistically accurate in its precise use of language. It should also be technically accurate in its use of specialized terms whose meanings are based in the context of a technical discipline. Both kinds of accuracy of phrasing and of technical concept are of utmost importance in writing.

Clarity The document should have the clarity. It should be written in simple and direct sentences. While a preparing a document one must pay attention to the sentence and word order. It should be restrained and structurally very simple. Any technical term that you have used should be defined properly with clarity.

Conciseness The document should be concise, minimum words should be used to express the basic idea of a given topic. Always pay attention to the fact that the document is not wordy, and it does not digress from the actual topic. While writing each word should be weighed for its need in a given document

Coherence The text should be coherent, and it should develop its subject matter in an easy-to-follow line of thinking. To achieve this, you can add the linkages like- 'in addition to', 'this process,' 'the first component,' and 'the second component', 'coming to the conclusion' etc.

Appropriateness Finally, the text should be appropriate to its purpose of presenting a general description for the non-expert readers as well as technical to the point that it remains a technical document which follows the requirements of your discipline.

4.1.1 Revising Content

When you are satisfied with the drafting and organisation of your document, review it to ensure that all the information is accurate, complete, and comprehensible. In addition to this, check to see that the information is relevant to your purpose and use.

4.1.2 How to revise your draft

Read through your draft slowly, stopping at the end of each section, and ask yourself the following questions:

- Is the information accurate?

- Is the information complete?
- Is any irrelevant information included in the document?
- Is the information comprehensible to your readers?

If you find there are inconsistencies, follow these steps:

- Correct any inaccurate quantitative data or other information.
- Add further information, explanations of concepts and processes.
- Delete from the document any information that is unnecessary and unimportant. If the information is important but does not go along the body of the document, include it in appendix.
- Clarify technical terms.
    a. Replace any term that is used incorrectly.
    b. Replace any vague or ambiguous terms.
    c. If two or more terms are used to refer to a single item, choose the best term and replace all occurrences of the other terms with the one you have selected.
    d. The first time you use an acronym or an abbreviation which may not be familiar to all your readers, write out the complete term followed by the acronym or abbreviation in parentheses.
    e. Consider adding a glossary if you use many terms with which some readers may not be familiar.

4.1.3 Proofreading An important stage in writing a document is to proofread it to avert any chances of typographical or grammatical error. People generally do not pay attention to it, but this is the final step in preparing a document/ draft.

While planning a document whether it is for report writing, assignment, proposal writing for business purposes or writing a research proposal- it involves several key steps to ensure clarity, coherence, and effectiveness. Here's a structured approach one should keep in mind while planning and preparing a document.

1. **Define the Purpose**
    - Clearly articulate the purpose of the report. What do you aim to achieve by writing it? Is it to inform, persuade, recommend, or analyze?
2. **Identify the Audience**
    - Understand who will be reading the report. Their level of expertise, interests, and expectations will influence your tone, style, and level of detail.
3. **Gather Information**
    - Collect all relevant data, research findings, and any other information necessary to address the report's purpose.
4. **Outline the Structure**
    - Create a clear outline that organizes the content logically. Typically, a report includes sections such as an introduction, background/context, methodology (if applicable), findings/results, discussion/analysis, conclusions, and recommendations.

5. **Introduction**
    - Start with a brief overview of the report's purpose and scope. Provide context to help readers understand the significance of the topic.
6. **Body**
    - Develop each section of the report based on the outline. Present information in a logical sequence, using headings and subheadings to guide the reader through the content. Support your points with evidence and analysis.
7. **Conclusion**
    - Summarize the key findings and insights from the report. Restate the main purpose and highlight any implications or recommendations.
8. **Recommendations (if applicable)**
    - If the report includes recommendations, present them clearly and justify why they are appropriate based on the findings.
9. **References**
    - Include a list of sources cited in the report. Follow the appropriate citation style (e.g., APA, MLA) and ensure accuracy and consistency.
10. **Appendices (if needed)**
    - Attach any supplementary materials, such as raw data, charts, graphs, or additional analysis, in appendices. Make sure to reference them in the main body of the report if necessary.
11. **Review and Revise**
    - Proofread the document for clarity, coherence, grammar, and spelling errors. Consider seeking feedback from colleagues or peers to improve the quality of the report.
12. **Finalize and Distribute**
    - Make any final adjustments and ensure the document is formatted correctly. Then, distribute the report to the intended audience through the appropriate channels.

4.2 Mechanics of Writing: Paragraphs and Punctuation

4.2.1 Paragraph Writing

A well composed paragraph has three essential elements.

- Topic sentence
- Controlling or governing idea
- Conclusion which will summarise the content of the paragraph and connect this paragraph to the next one.

Topic Sentences-Governing Idea-Conclusion

The topic sentence states the central idea of a paragraph. It is a key element in developing a unified and coherent paragraph. Although the topic sentence may appear anywhere in the paragraph, it is most often the first sentence. A topic statement may also contain an element of transition from the previous paragraph to give a continuity to the entire document. The next part of a paragraph is the idea which reflects the topic of the paragraph. This part should elaborate on the topic sentence with relevant information and evidence. In other words, the idea which dominates or governs the theme becomes the body of the paragraph. The last part of a paragraph is the concluding sentence which contains the final remarks of the arguments present in the body of the paragraph. This part is important because it introduces the idea and direction of the next paragraph.

4.2.2 Paragraph Development

Paragraphs can be developed in a variety of pattern that reflects your thinking and the requirements of the topic. As you write the topic sentence and its supporting sentences, look for ways to structure your thinking. More than one pattern of development may be used in a series of paragraphs.

Here are some important modes of paragraph development:

- Narration
- Process
- Description
- Comparison and contrast
- Analogy
- Cause and Effect

1. **Narration**

   Use **narration** to establish a series of events that tells the reader what happened. Narration follows a chronological pattern of development. It is a convincing mode of composing a paragraph to the extent that it tells a coherent story. This pattern or timeline is usually very easy to understand.

2. **Process**

   Use **process** in paragraphs to develop sequences that describe how an action is carried out or how something works.

3. **Description**

   Use descriptive prose to provide a physical picture or a functional view of the subject. Physical description develops a picture by identifying the shapes, materials, position, and functions of its subject. Such prose often serves as the raw material for more elaborate forms of analytical prose.

4. **Comparison and contrast**

   Use comparison and contrast to develop a topic by examining its similarities or dissimilarities to the other corresponding topic, process, or state. Comparison emphasizes the similarities whereas contrast, the differences. A paragraph may use both comparison and contrast.

5. **Analogy**

   Use analogy to explain one object or process in terms of another. The aptness of the analogy is generally a point of subtle judgment. Some analogies are more valid than others.

6. **Cause and Effect**

   Use cause and effect in paragraphs when you are tracking the development of one situation or event out of another. Cause and effect are an analytical mode of composing a paragraph. It attempts to show how events are influenced by or caused by others--the linkage of causation.

   The conclusion, being the last line of the paragraph, should be written in such a way that it connects the entire paragraph with the topic sentence of the next paragraph. In this way continuity and coherence is achieved.

4.3 Punctuation

Punctuation marks give meaning to a sentence. Imagine if you do not use any punctuation marks while preparing your assignment. Do you think it will be meaningful without punctuation marks? No, absolutely not! The punctuation marks give meaning, depth, and dimension to your writing.

Here are different punctuation marks that we use:

- Commas
- Semi-colon
- Colon
- Full stop
- Apostrophe
- Question marks
- Exclamation marks
- Hyphen

1. **Commas (,)** are used to break up different parts of a sentence. They allow someone to make sense of what they are reading. Commas occur where ideas are grouped, so that it become easier to understand these ideas. It may be helpful to think of commas as places where a reader might draw a breath. The comma forms a natural place in a sentence where the reader can pause, to make sense of an

idea. As comma signifies a pause, it follows natural speech pattern. Here are some of the ways it can be used.

- *To separate words in a list*

  Example He lost his purse, his money, his cards, and his pen.

- *To separate parts of a sentence*

  Example Firstly, I would like to consider the merits of an open-book exam. Secondly, I want to understand how to administer this kind of exam.

  Here the comma separates the first word from the body of the sentence, to indicate that this idea is only the first.

- *To separate two parts of a linked idea*

  Example After the examination had taken place, many students were concerned about the setting of a tough question paper.

- *To separate a final phrase, which is an afterthought*

  Example Few people enjoy working in a factory, especially on Saturdays.

2. **Semi-Colon (;)**

   The semi-colon contains a comma and a full stop. It may be helpful to think of semi-colons as halfway between the two. They are used in the following ways:

   - *To link sentences that are closely related*

     Example The metro came a little late; I realised it only when I reached my office late by half an hour.

     A full stop between the two sentences would detract from realisation that I reached my office late today, and a comma would not make enough of a break to allow the reader to make sense of the two ideas.

   - The semi-colon is also used **to link sentences that are in opposition to each other and to separate items in a list.**

3. **Colon (:)**

   When a colon is used in a sentence, the parts it separates do not need to be complete sentences in their own right. Colons are used in the following ways:

   - **To introduce a list**

     Example The stream-wise results of the AISSE examination conducted by the CBSE are as follows: Arun topped the.....

- The colon is also used **To link two sentences thematically and to draw out a conclusion:**

Here, what is said in the first sentence is contextualised by what is said in the second sentence.

- To show that letters are missing. This is known as **contraction.**
- To indicate ownership. This is known as **possession.**

4. **Apostrophes (')**

They are also used to show that something belongs to something else.

Example

- The boy's bag - means that the bag is owned by the boy.
- The boy's bags - means that the boy owns more than one bag.
- The boys' bag - means that the boys all share ownership of one bag.
- The boys' hats - means that the boys own several bags (or one each).

As you can see, the apostrophe usually comes before the 's' if the subject is single (the boy's), and after 's' if it is plural (the boys'). However, it may be different if the word for a single subject end with 's'. One useful way to deal with this is to see if the 's' is pronounced.

If the 's' is pronounced, there will be an additional 's' with the apostrophe before.

If the 's' is not pronounced, there will be no additional 's' and the apostrophe goes after the final 's'.

5. **Full stop** (.) also called the **period** is chiefly used to mark the end of a sentence expressing a statement, as in the following examples:

- I went to the market to buy a book.
- I have placed an order with Amazon for a book.

6. A **question mark** (?) is placed at the end of a sentence which is a direct question. Here are some examples:

- What is the capital of Andhra Pradesh?
- What did he tell you?

If the question is a direct quotation repeating the speaker's exact words, a question mark is still used:

Example 'Where did she go?' Arun asked me.

But a question mark is **not** used in an indirect question, in which the speaker's exact words are not repeated:

Example She asked if I had a pen she could borrow.

7. The **exclamation mark** (!) is used at the end of a sentence or a short phrase which expresses very strong feeling. Here are some examples:

   What a lovely view at the Rashtrapati Bhawan!
   That's fantastic!
   Help!
   Good heavens!
   Aah!
   Good riddance!

8. The **hyphen** (-) is the small bar found on every keyboard. It has several related uses; in every case, it is used to show that what it is attached to does not make up a complete word by itself. A hyphen is also used to indicate that a long word has been broken off at the end of a line:

   Example We were happy to find our pet lying oblivious in my *neigh-bour's* garden.

4.4 Plagiarism and Citation

Plagiarism is presenting the words or ideas of someone else as your own without proper acknowledgment of the source. When you write your assignment or work on a research paper, you take reference from a lot of resources. Taking reference and quoting from different resources that you have used is allowed and acceptable, but you must cite the source of the reference used. This is like crediting them for their original idea. Even when you summarize or paraphrase information found in books, articles, or Web pages, you must acknowledge the original author.

Why should we cite reference?
As it-

- **is the right thing to do** to give credit to those who had the idea
- **shows that you have read and understand** what experts have had to say about your topic
- **helps people find the sources** that you used in case they want to read more about the topic or if they want to cross check your content
- **provides evidence** for your arguments
- **is professional and standard practice** for students and scholars

A citation identifies for the reader the original source for an idea, information, or image that is referred to in a work. There are different styles of citations like APA, MLA, Chicago Manual Style etc. it depends on the discipline of enquiry as well. When you are citing something, ensure that you are following only one style at a time and not mixing two or more styles. Though there are many styles of citation, but each style will give you an information on the following:

Name of the author/s
Title of the book/article/research paper
Year of publication
Place of publication
Edition
Publishing house

It is crucial to follow only one citation style at a time when citing sources to ensure consistency, clarity, and professionalism in academic writing. Mixing multiple citation styles within a single document can lead to confusion for readers and may undermine the credibility of the research. By adhering to a single citation style throughout the document, writers maintain uniformity and make it easier for readers to locate and verify the sources cited.

Each citation style typically includes specific information about the source being cited. Common elements found in most citation styles include the name(s) of the author(s), title of the work (book, article, or research paper), year of publication, place of publication, edition (if applicable), and publishing house. Additionally, citation styles may require supplementary information such as page numbers for direct quotations or DOI (Digital Object Identifier) for online sources.

Some examples of citation styles used in academic writing include:

1. **APA (American Psychological Association) Style:** Widely used in the social sciences, APA style emphasizes clarity and conciseness. It includes author-date citations and a reference list at the end of the document.
2. **MLA (Modern Language Association) Style:** Commonly used in humanities disciplines such as literature and language studies, MLA style features in-text citations with author-page numbers and a Works Cited page.
3. **Chicago Manual of Style:** This style is flexible and used in various disciplines. It offers two documentation systems: notes and bibliography (commonly used in history and the humanities) and author-date (commonly used in the sciences).

By understanding the requirements and conventions of these citation styles, writers can effectively attribute credit to sources and maintain the integrity of their academic work.

4.5 Writing Short Proposals and Reports

Among the different kinds of communication challenges faced by a professional, the writing of proposals and reports is of prime significance. The report is one of the most detailed and complex forms of written communication that is undertaken in an organization and involves major investment in terms of time and money.

In this section, you will learn how to master the skill of proposal and report writing. A proposal or a report is normally a solicited communication and calls upon all your skills for its presentation. It is, therefore, appropriate that you should learn this, since you now have learnt all the techniques of effective communication and can use them to write a proposal or a report that meets all the organizational needs for which it has been solicited. *Business English, 2011.*

To facilitate your understanding of the process of writing proposals and reports, you need to first understand what they are, and when and why they are written. As you begin this section, you will see how proposals/reports fundamentally fulfill the needs of information and analysis and help management to take decisions regarding policies, procedures, and future plans. Since your document will have a long-term impact, you thus need to plan carefully before you begin drafting it.

The process of proposal/report writing can be summed up by the acronym RAP-Research, Analysis and Presentation. All three stages are equally important and each of them has been discussed in detail in this section.

4.5.1 Short Proposals and Reports

Pre Reading Activity

- What does the word 'proposal' suggest to you?
- How would you make/communicate a proposal-verbally or in writing?
- Usually, a short report is prepared and read on the college annual day. What is it about?
- Have you read a report published by any company?
- Did you find it interesting? Do reports contain only facts and figures?

Proposals

Proposals are meant to persuade. They are broadly categorized into research proposals and business proposals. Commonly, research proposals are submitted by/to academic institutions while business proposals come from business concerns. They are formal documents which may be solicited or unsolicited.

4.5.1.1 Solicited and Unsolicited Proposals

When a customer/client requires something that is not easy to procure from store/vendor then s/he sends a "Request for Proposal" or RFP, which contains a description of the product(s) / service(s) desired. **A solicited proposal is one which is sent in response to an RFP. An unsolicited proposal is one sent to customers even though they have not asked for it.**

When you write a solicited proposal it should contain and conform to the proposal requirements of the customer. You should meticulously follow formal instructions (if specified), provide information about product/ services to be delivered by you and deadlines to be met along with other specifications. As far as possible, use language which is similar to the one used by the solicitor and an outline which conforms to the specified guidelines. Similarly, when you write an unsolicited proposal, you should write in a manner which convinces the reader or the review committee that you are competent and qualified to solve their problem or execute their project.

4.5.1.2 Parts of a Proposal

1. **Cover letters** should be addressed to your client and state the purpose. It should also state the solutions you will find and how they are going to benefit the company. It should include the proposal title, name of the representative with designation, signature, and date.

2. **Title page** should include the proposal title, name of the person or company to whom you are submitting your proposal, as well as the name of the person submitting the proposal and date. If organizations specify certain information to be included in the title page, then make sure you do so.

3. **Executive summary** is one of the most important parts of the proposal. It should summarize the objectives of the proposal, and the procedures to be followed.

4. **Table of contents** and list of figures are required in proposals.

5. **Introduction** contains the purpose which should be stated in infinitive form given in the example.

   To supply…

   To bid for…

   To provide...

   To recommend…

The introduction should also clearly show that you have understood their problem(s) and the way you will tackle it/them. The scope of your project should be defined in your introduction as to the areas it will address. A long proposal contains a list of individuals who would work on the project. Some short proposals, too, have this list.

6. **Background** usually contains information on previous work/projects completed, evaluation of related projects and a statement showing how you plan to undertake this project based on your experience of already completed projects. In short proposals the background is usually omitted.

7. **Procedures** show your plan for meeting the requirements of the client. This is a statement of work describing what you would do or provide to her/ him. It should also have an implementation schedule, and a description of the products/services offered.

8. **Equipment and facilities** will describe the facilities required for the project and provide the needed facts and figures.

9. **Management plan** which will state how work will be organized and performed. A schedule of achieving milestones and allocation of resources should be provided; many companies specify how the budget should be presented. Try to adhere to it. You should also include a 'budget justification' to provide a rationale for your expenses.

10. **Appendices** contain additional matter like visuals and letters of recommendation and endorsement. This section may, at times, cause a negative reaction in the reader as being extraneous matter. This may be left out of short proposals usually contain the following.

How to Write an Effective Proposal

Before writing a proposal, ask yourself the following questions:

- Who is your customer and what is the requirement?
- Why do you think you are better than your competitors?
- How do you propose to deliver the product/service?
- Who will be involved in the delivery?
- When do you propose to deliver what you have promised?
- How will the customer benefit? How long would you take to deliver the goods/services?
- Where will the work be done? Where do you intend to deliver?
- When will the project start? When would the milestones be achieved? When will the project be complete? When will payments be due?

4.5.2 Short Reports

The basic functional areas of reports in an organization are as follows:

4.5.2.1 Informational functions

- Monitoring and controlling organizational processes.
- Implementation of policies.
- Complying with legal, procedural, and regulatory provisions.
- Create a document-base for future reference.

4.5.2.2 Analytical functions

- Help in decision-making by providing background details.
- Persuade others with information and assessment, through survey reports.

A few important points may be kept in mind while preparing a report

- That a report is usually documentation after an event or activity, thus the use of past tense is recommended.
- That a report is often solicited, that is, someone has asked for the report to be prepared. Thus, the tone used is formal.
- A report should have conclusions, be they suggestions, recommendations or simply advice, as per the purpose of the report.

In this section we shall discuss the short report, its format, style, and purpose. Short reports are usually less than five pages and do not need the elaborate outlines and structuring of the long report. The three basic sub-sections are introduction, investigation, and conclusion. Simple headings and sub-headings help the reader to follow through the text of the short report. Avoid using a running text. Instead, break up the text in terms of its thematic units. This would also help the report from becoming visually tedious.

4.5.2.3 Preparing a Report

A good short report will require both clarity and objectivity so that the reader of the report can see things the way you have mapped the main issues. A five-step formula may be adopted while preparing the report.

- **Planning**
- **Research**
- **Drafting**
- **Editing**
- **Concluding/Recommending**

Step 1: Planning- Depending on the terms of reference, that is, the task set out or the purpose of the report, plan the basic areas of the report. It is useful to study the issue(s) in context and arrive at a logical plan of action. Develop a working outline of the report and research.

Step II: Research- It is both primary and secondary, in primary research data is collected by you directly, as in the case of surveys. In secondary research, you use the studies conducted by others. In the latter case, it is important that you reveal and acknowledge the sources. If you do not, it is a form of stealing, called plagiarism. Research may require Internet-use, questionnaires, oral interaction with members at the workplace, etc. Suitable communication strategies become important so that the right kind of information can be collected.

Step III: Drafting- this step helps you putting together in a written format all the data that you have gathered. Follow the working plan that you had prepared in Step 1. It will help you in organizing your data. Also, see that you are stacking your points in a manner that leads to a logical outcome, your conclusion/recommendation.

Step IV: Editing- Sometimes considered less important, this step is vital to the actual report presentation. Edit and revise so that no relevant mention is left out or irrelevant included. This fine-tuning is necessary to keep the report focused. If need be, visual representation, graphs, statistical etc., may be incorporated. Choose the desired tone quality. Substantiate any claims that you may make. The basic purpose of editing is to meet the twin requirements of clarity and objectivity.

Step-V: Concluding/Recommending- although all reports may not expect you to come up with recommendations, conclusions are more than just formalities. In this section you will interpret the data, and in conclusion, recall the objectives of the report and mention how you have realized them. Recommendations are to be included if specifically asked for.

Seven Errors that can Undermine Your Report

1. *Lack of objectivity-*

   Seeing only the facts that support your view and ignoring any contradictory formation.

2. *Hasty generalizations forming judgments based on insufficient evidence or special cases.*

3. *Hidden assumptions hiding a questionable major premise.*

4. *Either-or scenarios Setting up two alternatives and not allowing for others.*

5. *False causal relationships assuming that event A caused event B only because A preceded B*

6. *Begged questions assuming as proven what you are going to prove.*

7. *Personal attacks or appeals to popular prejudice Sinking people or ideas you do not like by chaining them to irrelevant but un- popular actions or ideas. (Bovee et al, 2006).*

- Proposals can be written for purposes of research or business.
- Business proposals can be solicited or unsolicited.
- There are several components of a proposal.
- You must plan before writing a persuasive proposal.
- Reports perform two basic functions-informational functions and analytical functions.
- While preparing a report, you must use the five-step formula-planning.
- Research, drafting, editing and concluding. Use past tense and a formal tone in writing reports.

4.6 Outline and Organization of Long Reports

4.6.1 Purpose of a Business Report

It provides a detailed report of the situation, a problem or of the action taken or the findings of an investigation. Based on such reports, the management of a company can arrive at decisions regarding policy matters, with full knowledge of the background facts and circumstances.

A report is also written to justify the policies, need for action, and decisions taken in controversial situations.

The report also gives information about a company's activities, progress, plans and problems.

4.6.2 Types of Report

Reports are broadly of two kinds:

- **Formal reports**
- **Semi-formal/informal reports.**

Reports are also classified according to their purpose and their form. Some of them are:

- **Routine reports** (based on frequency) are made by filling in a printed form and submitting them on a recurring and periodic basis.
- Depending upon the intended reader, reports may be **internal** (designed for use within an organization) and **external** reports that are sent to people outside the organization.
- Based on length, there are **short reports** that are generally of one to nine pages and **long reports** that are of 10 or more pages. The former may analyze just one

aspect of the problem and not require any formal research, whereas the latter examines a problem in detail and requires more extensive research and preparation time.

- Based on intent, reports have been divided into **informational reports** and **analytical reports**. Informational reports present facts and data without analysis or recommendations. They provide information to readers. Analytical reports are written to solve a problem that convinces readers that the decisions and recommendations reached by the management are justified based on data analysis and interpretations presented in such reports.

- **Informational Reports**

  These include reports for monitoring and controlling operations, statements of policies and procedures, compliance reports, and progress reports.

  Reports for Monitoring and Controlling Operations These reports must be accurate, thorough and honest. They highlight problems and report achievements.

  Reports for Implementing Policies and Procedures These reports give information in a straightforward manner. Some of them are preserved as guidelines for future purposes, while others are one-time papers.

  Reports for Complying with Government Regulations These reports are written in response to regulations imposed by government agencies. The regulatory agency gives instructions on how to write the necessary reports. It is, therefore, important to be honest, thorough, and accurate.

  Reports for Documenting Progress Some reports are written for the sake of mere formality while others are vital in client relationships. They are submitted on a regular basis for documentation.

- **Analytical Reports**

  Company heads also rely upon additional information, analysis and suggestions provided in analytical reports to take decisive measures. Hence, such reports require a correct representation of facts along with good insight and excellent communication skills.

  Problem-solving Reports In order to arrive at decisions, heads of companies need basic information as well as rigorous analysis of the problem. These reports provide just the kind of information that is based on primary and secondary research.

4.6.3 Terms of Reference

Whenever a report is required to be written, an individual or a team is assigned to the task. The scope, purpose, subject and time-limit of the report is prescribed by the one who wants the report to be prepared. One could follow a useful pattern like this:

To report on... (Subject)... as requested by... (Name and designation) on... (Date)... (Taylor 2005)

The process of writing a report is left to the writer. To write a report, the writer must conduct research and analysis. S/he must first investigate the problem, look for facts, collect evidence for the facts observed, and then analyze them before presenting observations, conclusions, and suggestions as solutions to the problem. There are different methods available to the writer for conducting research, namely, visits, interviews, questionnaires, data banks, studying records of the organization, consulting existing literature and documents as relevant sources of information. The writer also needs to know the background and the context of the subject s/he is investigating. Hence, a study of the background and collection of data are a necessary component of report writing (*Chaturvedi and Chaturvedi, 2004*).

4.6.4 Outline of Long Reports

Formal long reports have the following elements

1. **Cover page/Title fly:** It generally contains the number and the date.

2. **Title page.** The title page repeats the title of the report and gives some more information. In brief, the title page consists of the following information:

   Title of the report (short and unambiguous)
   The name/s of person/s who prepared the report.
   The name/s of person/s or organization who/which authorized the report.
   Date of submission.

3. **Letter of transmittal:** This reads like a preface to a book. It is written in the first person using personal pronouns and in an informal style. It talks about the different issues handled by the report. It includes information about the scope of the report, the methods used for the findings, and drawbacks or limitations, if any. It also highlights the major findings of the report, necessary details, the conclusion, and the recommendations. It acknowledges the help extended by other people in completing the report and thanks those who gave them the opportunity to undertake the assignment.

4. **Table of contents:** It is a kind of a map describing the structure of the report. It is an outline of the report, indicating the coverage, sequence, and hierarchical importance of the information in the report. The different topics in the report are identified with their page numbers for easy access and reference. You should be careful to list the contents with their relevant headings in the same order as they

appear in the report to avoid confusion. If there are very few visuals, they can be put in the content list, otherwise they should be listed separately. The table of contents is an important document because it helps people to locate specific information in an otherwise long report.

5. **Executive summary:** This is placed just after the table of contents. It is an overview of the complete report, summarizing the salient features of the document including the introduction or the findings, the recommendations, the conclusions and relevant illustrations of charts, graphs, and pie diagrams if any. Busy executives prefer reading the executive summary rather than the long report to get a preview of the report.

   It covers all the major points of the report including the structure, purpose, methods, and overall significance. 'A good executive summary opens a window into the body of the report and allows the reader to quickly see how well you have managed your message'. (*Bovee et al, 2006*)

6. **The actual report:** The actual report has three parts to it. They are introduction, body, and conclusion.

   Introduction

   - **Purpose of the report:** It tells us the main objectives of the report and its need.
   - **The terms of reference:** It briefly describes the scope of the report, its contents and limitations or problems faced, if any.
   - **Research methods:** It refers to the different methods used to collect data, like sampling, fieldwork, and questionnaires. It also tells us whether the data collected is from primary or secondary sources or both, and the different statistical tools used for analysis.

   Body

   It gives a detailed discussion of the results of the investigation using the different research tools. A lot of data in the form of graphs, charts and tables help in understanding the details of the report. Avoid being prosaic and substantiate the findings with visual inputs for better comprehension. The body of the report is divided into several sections which are further sub-divided into sub-sections. All of them will require headings and, therefore, use the numbering system of decimals to distinguish the different sections and sub-sections. This will help the reader to understand the report in a coherent manner and not get confused with sections and sub-sections.

   Conclusion

   This summarizes the main idea of the report and gives relevant recommendations. Use the SWOT (Strength, Weakness. Opportunities, Threats) analysis for recommendations.

- It also gives a detailed result of the investigation.
- It also answers all the questions raised in the report initially.
- It puts forward problems, if any, in achieving the objectives.
- It gives clear and definite recommendations.
- It briefly states the action to be taken.
- It states how it can help in any future course of action.

7. **Appendix:** This includes all the information and documents which you have used during your research while writing the report but is not directly connected with the report. Moreover, these documents may be very long and bulky and it would not be possible to include them in the main report. The information included in the appendix are sample questionnaires, statistical data, statistical formulas, copies of important documents used, other instruments of survey, etc. Each of the appendixes needs to be numbered and captioned. The documents need to be arranged in a logical sequence.

8. **Glossary:** It is a list of technical terms used in the report.

   It is arranged alphabetically.

   It explains how the words are used.

   It can also function as a dictionary.

   It gives rules for forming and abbreviating technical words.

9. **Bibliography.** It is a list of secondary sources used while preparing the report. All textual sources, whether published or unpublished, should be acknowledged. It is generally written in the following manner.

   The name(s) of the author-Title-Name of publisher- place of publication-Year of publication and edition if any.

10. **Index** It is a detailed listing of names, places, subjects, together with the page number where they are mentioned. It is organized in an alphabetical manner. A reader can locate information regarding any topic with the help of the index.

Unit Summary

In this unit, you have learnt about:

- *Planning the document- understanding the objectives*
- *Collecting information- forming the problem statement*
- *Writing introduction and the body of the draft*
- *Paragraph writing- topic sentence*
- *Punctuation marks*
- *Citation*
- *Plagiarism*

- *Citation styles/ in-house styles*
- *What a business report is*
- *About different kinds of business reports*
- *How to write a long business report (an outline)*

Exercises

Multiple Choice Questions

1. What is the first step in preparing any document?
   a. Writing the introduction
   b. Collecting appropriate materials
   c. Proofreading
   d. Composing a problem statement

2. Which of the following is NOT a consideration while writing the first draft of a document?
   a. Accuracy
   b. Clarity
   c. Complexity
   d. Conciseness

3. Which statement describes the importance of accuracy in document writing?
   a. Accuracy ensures the document is lengthy and detailed.
   b. Accuracy focuses on using ambiguous language.
   c. Accuracy is necessary for precise use of language and technical terms.
   d. Accuracy is irrelevant in technical documents.

4. What should be done with technical terms in a document?
   a. Avoid using them
   b. Define them properly
   c. Use them without explanation
   d. Use them in the introduction only

5. Which punctuation mark is used to introduce a list?
   a. Comma
   b. Semi-colon
   c. Colon
   d. Apostrophe

6. What is the purpose of punctuation marks in writing?
    a. To confuse the reader
    b. To add complexity to sentences
    c. To provide meaning and clarity
    d. To make the text visually appealing

7. What are the essential elements of a well-composed paragraph?
    a. Introduction, Body, Conclusion
    b. Thesis, Evidence, Conclusion
    c. Topic sentence, Controlling idea, Conclusion
    d. Theme, Plot, Resolution

8. Which mode of paragraph development focuses on explaining one object or process in terms of another?
    a. Narration
    b. Description
    c. Analogy
    d. Cause and Effect

9. What are the two main kinds of proposals?
    a. Formal and informal
    b. Solicited and unsolicited
    c. Business and academic
    d. Research and analytical

10. What is the purpose of a cover letter in a proposal?
    a. To summarize the main findings
    b. To list all the appendices
    c. To introduce the team members
    d. To state the purpose and solutions

Answers: 1-b, 2-c, 3-c, 4-b, 5-c, 6-c, 7-c, 8-c, 9-b, 10-d

Subjective Questions

1. Define 'Accuracy' and 'coherence' in the context of document writing.
2. What is meant by 'Clarity' and 'conciseness' when preparing a document?
3. Differentiate between "Proofreading" and "Revising" in the context of document preparation.
4. Why is planning important in the preparation of documents? Explain the structured approach of preparing the document.
5. When and why should you review your document? Mention the steps that you should follow if you find inconsistencies in your draft.
6. Describe the function of a "topic sentence" in a paragraph. What is the purpose of narration in paragraph development, and what pattern does it typically follow?
7. Define Punctuation marks. What is the use of exclamation mark? Explain with example.
8. Why is it important to follow only one citation style at a time when citing sources? What information does each citation style typically include? Mention some examples of citation styles used in academic writing.
9. What is report? Explain the purpose of the executive summary in a report and its importance for busy executives.
10. Define the purpose of a cover letter in a proposal and explain its components.

Know More

- *Historical records indicate that document planning may be traced back to prehistoric civilisations. Prior to their hieroglyphic scripts, the Egyptians used careful planning.*
- *Precision in technical writing includes both factual correctness and the meticulous use of language to ensure that each word is used in its precise context.*
- *As highlighted by Aristotle, Clarity is the paramount principle in writing since it is the most crucial attribute of effective communication.*
- *Shakespeare's famous phrase "Brevity is the soul of wit " emphasises conciseness," underscoring the need for brevity in effective communication.*
- *Coherence refers to the quality of a written work where all its components are logically related, facilitating the readers' comprehension of the argument or story.*

- *Relevance is essential to customise the document to match the audience's knowledge and engagement. For instance, a technical publication tailored for engineers will exhibit substantial differences compared to one designed for the general public.*
- *Proofreading is a long-standing activity that originated in the early days of printing. During this time, proofreaders would meticulously examine printed texts by hand to identify and correct any flaws.*
- *Various cultures exhibit distinct approaches to developing paragraphs. Japanese literature often employs a circular form, concluding by returning to the primary topic.*
- *The development of punctuation marks has taken place across many generations. The comma was first used by an Italian printer, Aldus Manutius, in the 15th century.*
- *Plagiarism, or using another person's work without recognising it, dates back to ancient Roman times. Nonetheless, over the twentieth century, formal citation styles such as APA and MLA emerged to provide a uniform system for academic writing.*

References and Suggested Readings

Bentley, T. (2002). *Report writing in business*. Elsevier.

Schneider, W. J., Lichtenberger, E. O., Mather, N., & Kaufman, N. L. (2018). *Essentials of assessment report writing*. John Wiley & Sons.

Young, D. J. (2009). *The mechanics of writing*. Dog Ear Publishing.

DYNAMIC QR CODING FOR FURTHER READINGS

Mechanics of writing

Business Report: Structure

Business Proposal

REFERENCES

- *Anderson, P. V. (2013). Technical Communication. New Delhi: Cengage Learning Pvt Ltd.*
- *Baude, D. M. (2006). The Executive Guide to E-mail Correspondence: Including Model Letters for Every Situation. Red Wheel/Weiser.*
- *Bentley, T. (2002). Report writing in business. Elsevier.*
- *Bovee, C. L., Thill, J. V., & Schatzman, B. E. (2006). Business communication today. Pearson Education.*
- *Business English. (2011). University of Delhi. Delhi. Pearson Education.*
- *Chaturvedi, P. D., & Chaturvedi, M. (2004). Business Communication: Concepts, Cases and Applications. Singapore: Pearson Education.*
- *Comer, D. E. (2018). The Internet book: everything you need to know about computer networking and how the Internet works. New York: Chapman and Hall/CRC.*
- *Coulmas, F. (2013). Sociolinguistics: The Study of Speakers' Choices (2 ed.). New York: Cambridge University Press.*
- *Courtland L Bovee, J. V. (2006). Business Communication Today. Pearson Education.*
- *Downes, C. (2009). Cambridge English For Job-Hunting. Cambridge University Press.*
- *Duck, S., & McMahon, D. T. (2012). Basics of Communication; A Relational Perspective. SAGE.*
- *Ferguson, S., & Ferguson, S. D. (1980). Intercom; Readings in Organizational Communication. Hayden Book Company.*
- *Fiske, J. (2011). Introduction to Communication Studies. Routledge.*
- *Hartley, P., & Bruckmann, C. G. (2002). Business Communication. London: Routledge.*
- *Holliday, A., Hyde, M., & Kullman, J. (2021). Intercultural communication: An advanced resource book for students. Routledge.*
- *Katz, D., & Kahn, R. L. (1978). The Social Psychology of Organizations. Wiley.*
- *Koontz, H., O'Donnell, C., & Weihrich, H. (1980). Management. McGraw-Hill.*
- *Kulkarni, M. M. (2006). Modern Business Communication. New Delhi: R. Chand and Co.*
- *McMurrey, & Buckley. (2008). Handbook for Technical Writing. Cengage Learning.*
- *Monippally, M. (2001). Business Communication Strategies. New Delhi: McGraw-Hill Education (India) Pvt Limited.*
- *Murphy, H. A., Hildebrandt, H. W., & Thomas, J. P. (n.d.). Effective Business Communications. 1997: McGraw-Hill.*
- *Newstrom, J. W. (2011). Organizational Behavior: Human Behavior at Work. McGraw-Hill/Irwin.*
- *Nicholls, A. (2006). Master Public Speaking. Jaico Publishing House.*
- *Quintanilla, K. M., & Wahl, S. T. (2018). Business and professional communication: Keys for workplace excellence (4 ed.). SAGE Publications.*
- *Raman, M., & Sharma, S. (2015). Technical Communication; Principles and Practices. Oxford University Press.*
- *Rani, D. S. (2010). Advanced Communication Skills Laboratory Manual. Pearson Education.*

- *Schneider, W. J., Lichtenberger, E. O., Mather, N., & Kaufman, N. L. (2018). Essentials of Assessment Report Writing (2 ed.). Wiley.*
- *Sen, L. (2007). Communication Skills. New Delhi: PHI Learning.*
- *Sharma, R. C., & Mohan, K. (2017). Business Correspondence and Report Writing: A Practical Approach to Business & Technical Communication. Tata McGraw-Hill.*
- *Thomas, N. (2007). The John Adair Handbook of Management and Leadership. New Delhi: Viva Books Private Limited.*
- *Tomalin, & Thomas. (2009). International English for Call Centres. Macmillan Publishers.*
- *Tyagi, K., & Misra, P. (2011). Basic Technical Communication. New Delhi: PHI Learning.*
- *Viswamohan. (2007). English For Technical Communication (For First Yr Engg Students). McGraw-Hill Education (India) Pvt Limited.*
- *Weiss, E. H. (2005). The elements of international English style: A guide to writing correspondence, reports, technical documents, and internet pages for a global audience. New York: Routledge.*
- *Whittaker, J. (2002). The Internet. Routledge.*
- *Young, D. J. (2006). Foundations of Business English: An Integrative Approach. New Delhi: Tata McGraw-Hill.*
- *Young, D. J. (2009). The Mechanics of Writing. Writer's Toolkit Publishing, LLC.*

CO-PO Attainment Table

Course outcomes (COs) for this course can be mapped with the programme outcomes (POs) after the completion of the course and a correlation can be made for the attainment of POs to analyze the gap. After proper analysis of the gap in the attainment of POs necessary measures can be taken to overcome the gaps.

Table for CO and PO attainment

Course Outcomes	Attainment of Programme Outcomes (1- Weak Correlation; 2- Medium correlation; 3- Strong Correlation)							
	PO-1	PO-2	PO-3	PO-4	PO-5	PO-6	PO-7	PO-8
CO-1								
CO-2								
CO-3								
CO-4								
CO-5								
CO-6								

The data filled in the above table can be used for gap analysis.

INDEX